M000305613

Reducing Belly Fat
Reducing Medications
The Team Approach

To Uncle Oneil
MATTRUE
Thank you so Much!

2

Reducing Belly Fat
Reducing Medications
The Team Approach

Christopher Sylvain

Whole Life Press
New Orleans, La.

Whole Life Press
New Orleans, Louisiana

ISBN   978-0-578-23106-8

To my wife who I could never imagine life without. My friend, my supporter, my love. I am forever grateful.

To my wonderful children and theirs. I love and appreciate you eternally. Your input into this project has been invaluable. LaShonda, Aryane, Aisha, Tia, Christopher and Amber: Thank You.

To Faith: We love you!

The Quick Answer: QSS

Quit Sodas, Juices, Diet Drinks and Smoothies

Switch to Brown from White

Sweat Everyday

Q

Quit

Quit all sodas, juices, diet drinks, smoothies and processed sweets, as they all are unhealthy to the body. Drink water, tea, flavored water for drinks. Eat fruit as a snack. Honey is a non-processed sweetener that can be added to anything. It has over 200 ingredients and exhibits antidiabetic and antioxidant properties.[1] [2] The soda and junk food companies are trying to get you addicted to their processed chemicals. Fight back!

---

[1] "Traditional and Modern Uses of Natural ...."
https://www.ncbi.nlm.nih.gov/pmc/articles/PMC3758027/.
[2] "Honey: A Novel Antioxidant - NCBI." 12 Apr. 2012,
https://www.ncbi.nlm.nih.gov/pmc/articles/PMC6268297/.

What are sodas and processed sweets?

Any processed beverage or snack that has sugar or zero calorie sweeteners in them. Read the list of ingredients on the label and if it contains sugar, high fructose corn syrup, brown sugar, agave nectar, syrup, molasses, stevia, saccharin, aspartame, sucralose, sugar alcohols (such as maltitol and sorbitol), maltodextrin, or neotame, then avoid. Two 16 ounce sodas a day can lead to fatty liver disease and metabolic syndrome (high blood pressure, diabetes, and high cholesterol) in 6 months.[3]

---

[3] "Carbohydrate intake and nonalcoholic fatty liver disease - NCBI." https://www.ncbi.nlm.nih.gov/pmc/articles/PMC4405421/.

Food	Effects (abbreviated)	Result
Sodas	toxic to the gut and liver	belly fat
Diet sodas	weight gain	belly fat
Juices	same as sodas - damaged fiber so acts like a soda	belly fat
Smoothies	same as juices - damaged fiber so acts like a soda	belly fat
Cakes	insulin spike	belly fat
Pies	insulin spike	belly fat
Health bars	loaded with sugar therefore insulin spike	belly fat
Candy bars	insulin spike	belly fat
Candy	insulin spike	belly fat
Cookies	insulin spike	belly fat

S

Switch to Brown from White

Brown rice - white rice causes an insulin spike therefore increases belly fat.

Brown pasta - white pasta causes a small insulin spike therefore increases belly fat.

Brown bread - white bread causes a big insulin spike therefore increases belly fat. Insulin is truly not the only substance whose imbalances create dysfunction but it is representative.

Brown bread is a huge challenge because it is extremely rare to find brown bread without added sugar in the ingredients. Many of them contain whole grains mixed with refined grains and added sugars. This leads to them having more sugar than a Chips Ahoy cookie and will still be labeled as "whole wheat". Big food companies label them as whole grain to make them seem healthy...

S

Sweat daily. When you exercise aerobically, the belly fat goes away first. Sweat from a wheelchair, bed, walking or any activity that builds your heart rate. It is better at removing belly fat than weight lifting or balance exercises. Aerobic is best. Remember a little is better than none.

So remember to QSS:
Quit, Switch and Sweat and watch the belly fat go down....

Commit to 40 Days!

Nourishing the Total Man

The frontiers of theo/pharma/nutrition

Belly fat is a problem. A growing waistline that causes clothes to fit very tight and getting prescriptions for medications are the primary drivers to seeking better health. Having tried to solve these many times, most distrust any solutions except working out more and/or pushing away from the table. The problem is that it only works for a while then it comes back worse each time. Is God in this? Why doesn't God respond?

The quick answer is to pray, eat more S^fruits, vegetables, whole grains and of course exercise. If it were that simple, there wouldn't be a problem. You may see people work so hard to eat right and exercise only to see minimal change or remain ill. The whole cycle just doesn't seem to line up with a loving, kind God... The utter frustration, depression, illness and early death from people who are trying so hard seems to go against every concept of God that we have. The issue of why good people suffer is the pinnacle of the war between the cosmic struggle of good versus evil. Evil rarely raises its head openly but is subtle and disguised. What is really in the foods that we eat? How do they act in the body? Why are our waistlines continuing to grow? Why isn't God answering our prayers? Why is the church so unhealthy? Why are hard working, intelligent people continuing to fail at this? How can we get healthier? In this book, we will give you practical solutions and answers to reduce belly fat and reduce medications through the team approach.

First, we need to understand what is going on before we can move forward. It reminds me of when I was driving to speak at a conference 4 hours from home. Leaving about 4 o'clock in the morning, the drive was beautiful and peaceful. About 6 am the sun started rising from behind the car and I almost got into a wreck trying to look back to see. It was a long country road where the air was clean, trees were tall, and you knew God created it all. After looking back a few times, I realized that the sun actually did not rise. It can't rise - the sun doesn't move – it's a star and stars stay relatively still. Planets move and we're on this planet earth moving around the sun while spinning. It takes 24 hours at about 1000 miles per hour to spin a complete cycle and a year at 67,062 miles per hour to make it all around the sun. It just seemed like the sun was rising! That's like the body. There are fast, massive, unimaginable things going on inside the body that we cannot see or feel.

How Do Our Bellies Rise?

The conventional answer to our rising belly fat is that we eat too much. The primary problem is not how much, but what we eat. The belly rises predominantly when fat begins to accumulate around the internal organs, particularly the liver. This fat is deep inside the body where you can't pinch with your fingers. AB loungers, sit ups and other so called get a "six pack" exercises can't specifically target this fat. This is the fat that changes our shape. We can get larger and gain weight, but if it is proportional to the size of our body, it's no problem. The problem comes from losing our shape from increased belly fat whereas the rest of the body doesn't increase proportionally.[4]

Women move from a coke bottle shape to more like an apple shape. Men lose their "six pack" abs to gain a spare tire. The optimum waist to hip ratio for women is 0.7. To get yours, measure your waist and hips then

---

[4] "Waist circumference as a vital sign in clinical practice ... - Nature." 4 Feb. 2020, https://www.nature.com/articles/s41574-019-0310-7.

divide the hip measurement into the waist measurement. The closer to 0.7 a woman is, the more attractive she is to men provided all other factors are the same. The more a woman resembles 0.7, the more it activates the brain centers that drive the man's social appetite and attention towards that female.

The more "hourglass type" the woman's body is, the more likely she is to get pregnant, have mental and physical energy, have an easier childbirth and have a lower incidence of depression.[5] [6] Male attractiveness is related to facial and body symmetry (where everything is balanced out). We're only looking at physical attractiveness here.[7] A more masculine face indicates higher fertility in men just as femininity indicates higher estrogen levels and fertility in females and

[5] "Optimal Waist-to-Hip Ratios in Women Activate Neural ... - PLOS." 5 Feb. 2010, https://journals.plos.org/plosone/article?id=10.1371/journal.pone.0009042.

[6] "Body shape and women's attractiveness : The critical role of ...." https://www.ncbi.nlm.nih.gov/pubmed/24214368.

[7] "Sex Differences in Short-term Mate Preferences and ...." 8 Aug. 2007, https://research.vu.nl/ws/portalfiles/portal/2391742/Straaten+Archives+of+Sexual+Behavior+37+2008+u.pdf.

therefore attractiveness.[8] [9] The major areas of attractiveness are masculinity/femininity (sexual dimorphism), waist to hip ratio (females), body symmetry (males), facial symmetry and familiarity when health is not known. Once health is known then those attractiveness indicators are all diminished.[10] [11] [12] Waist to hip ratio (women's coke bottle likeness) being the primary indicator of health stands then as the strongest measurement of female attractiveness excluding looking at someone's medical records. For men, it's facial symmetry, shoulder to waist ratio but none are more important than kindness, power, or

[8] "Preferences across the Menstrual Cycle for ... - PLOS." 7 Jan. 2009, https://journals.plos.org/plosone/article?id=10.1371/journal.pone.0004138.

[9] "Sex Differences in Short-term Mate Preferences and ...." 8 Aug. 2007, https://research.vu.nl/ws/portalfiles/portal/2391742/Straaten+Archives+of+Sexual+Behavior+37+2008+u.pdf.

[10] "Perceived health contributes to the attractiveness of facial ...." https://www.ncbi.nlm.nih.gov/pubmed/17972486.

[11] "Attractiveness of Own-Race, Other-Race, and Mixed-Race ...." https://journals.sagepub.com/doi/10.1068/p5191.

[12] "Male facial appearance signals physical strength to women ...." https://onlinelibrary.wiley.com/doi/abs/10.1002/ajhb.20583.

finances. The effects of belly fat on men and women are different.

This belly has tremendous weight on it for our self-esteem, social acceptance, personal growth and health. What is so amazing is that its disproportionate growth is fueled mainly by substances that are new to us in these quantities. Man has created his own problem. As we eat these so called foods, they preferentially deposit viscerally (belly).[13]

These substances make the fat sick (adiposopathy) which leads to a vicious cycle. This sick fat becomes a living, active organ that discharges hormones that affect every area of the body. The cycle seems to be self perpetuating in that once the fat gets sick, it creates the conditions for more and more fat to store there with the belly growing and growing and the fat getting sicker and sicker... As the fat grows the belly grows, clothes no longer fit, we appear less attractive, and we are less healthy.

---

[13] "Carbohydrate intake and nonalcoholic fatty liver disease - NCBI." https://www.ncbi.nlm.nih.gov/pmc/articles/PMC4405421/.

Fat as a Fountain

This visceral fat then becomes the key changeable area of our lives. This fat around our internal organs isn't only a storage place, but also it spews out substances like a fountain on the inside of our body. Let's begin with fat itself. Fat secretes fat (free fatty acids).[14] This fat contributes to insulin resistance which means when you eat refined carbohydrates, it causes the body to use a large amount of insulin to move it out of the bloodstream and into the cells since the body is resistant to the insulin. So eventually when you eat a meal, particularly a high refined carbohydrate meal, the sugar will stay in the bloodstream. When you go to the doctor to get your sugar checked, the number will be high. Over time they may then say you have diabetes. It starts with the visceral (belly) fat.

---

[14] "Fat Depots, Free Fatty Acids, and Dyslipidemia - NCBI." 7 Feb. 2013, https://www.ncbi.nlm.nih.gov/pmc/articles/PMC3635208/.

Insulin also causes sugar to become fat (lipogenesis). Not only does fat secrete fat, but now more insulin turns the food we eat into fat. If you ever knew someone who was given "the needle" or insulin for diabetes, they usually gain weight. Insulin potently turns foods to fat so people then gain more weight. Where? Of course they gain it mainly close around the liver: the belly! Over time though, the beta cells of the pancreas, which secretes insulin, fail from overuse. It's like trying to run a car full speed for hours. Sooner or later the engine will fail from overuse. That's what happens to the beta cells of the pancreas.[15] By this time much of the damage is done with less and less insulin responding to more and more sweets attempting to move more and more glucose into cells that are more and more resistant. No wonder we have blood sugars as high as 275 mg/dl. First, doctors will start you on metformin, a common medication to lower your blood sugar to address the insulin resistance then possibly give glyburide later to get more insulin to the bloodstream. This only lasts for

---

[15] "Beta-cell failure as a complication of diabetes. - NCBI - NIH." https://www.ncbi.nlm.nih.gov/pubmed/18777097.

a while, then insulin may be needed – unless we stop eating the "sugar"...

Substances Flowing From The Fountain

Leptin was thought to be the wonder hormone. It decreases food intake and body weight. Sounds great? It affects our desire for a certain quantity of food giving us the ability to hit the "all you can eat" restaurants with full control. It regulates our taste preferences allowing us to walk past the candy aisle with ease. It regulates how full we feel when we eat, so we just eat one bite if needed. It is purely the self control hormone.[16] Leptin also affects our metabolic rate, or how fast we burn calories. Some people can seem to just look at food and gain weight, but with a high metabolic rate we can eat more and weigh less. It regulates insulin and blood glucose levels like an antidiabetic hormone.[17] Once

---

[16] "Leptin, cardiovascular diseases and type 2 diabetes ... - NCBI."
7 Jun. 2018,
https://www.ncbi.nlm.nih.gov/pmc/articles/PMC6289384/.

[17] "Leptin signaling in adipose tissue: Role in lipid ... - NCBI - NIH." 22 Jun. 2012,
https://www.ncbi.nlm.nih.gov/pmc/articles/PMC3482005/.

discovered in 1994, everyone began looking for a leptin type drug. What could be better in the world! Well the problem is that in overweight people it doesn't work properly – all thunder and no rain. It seems to only work for thin people who appear to eat all they want and not gain weight. Someone else can appear to smell food and gain a pound. When this happens, it's called leptin resistance. As of now, the exact mechanism isn't understood, but obese people have high leptin levels which just shouldn't be so if leptin was working properly. With its actions being so many and so complex, it may take years to figure out how and why it fails.

Visceral fat spews out angiotensinogen which affects the system that controls blood pressure. There's a direct relationship between belly fat and high blood pressure. [18] Most people begin with hydrochlorothiazide 25 mg daily then move on to one or two more between 45 and 55 years old. We did about 100 blood pressures at

---

[18] "Comparisons of body mass index, waist ... - BMJ Open." https://bmjopen.bmj.com/content/10/1/e032874.

health fairs (in poor neighborhoods[19]) this year and only found 2 people within normal range. The blood pressure issue is similar to the guy that walks around an industrial plant with a clipboard in his hand. He usually makes more money than anyone except the executives, but he only checks pressures. If he doesn't do his job the whole plant could blow up from high pressure in the pipes. That's the way our bodies are. When the pressure is high the whole plant (kidneys, eyes, heart, etc...) can "blow up". We need our pressures checked...

Belly (visceral) fat secretes interleukin 6 which also causes insulin resistance, but this one increases inflammation which leads to atherosclerosis among other things. When you cut yourself you see this sticky puss. That's similar to what happens in our blood vessels when inflamed. Add in some cholesterol and you easily get a clot. So with more insulin in the bloodstream you get more fat and with more fat you get

---

[19] "Socioeconomic Inequalities in Disability-free Life Expectancy ...." 15 Jan. 2020, https://academic.oup.com/biomedgerontology/advance-article/doi/10.1093/gerona/glz266/5698372.

more inflammation and with more inflammation that cholesterol gets stuck in the vessels. Interleukin 6 is a powerful stimulator of C-reactive protein release from the liver which is an indicator of inflammation therefore cardiovascular disease and cancer risk. Levels of C-reactive protein can give us a view of the amount of inflammation caused by high interleukin 6 levels.

TNF-alpha is another inflammatory substance that also causes insulin resistance and there is also PAI-1 which helps the blood to clot more with TNF-alpha stimulating more PAI-1. More clots, more inflammation, and more insulin resistance all create a mountain of trouble inside the body with rarely any exterior symptoms. And it gets worse...

The next one we'll cover is adiponectin. This one is a great one that decreases insulin resistance and decreases inflammation but the problem is that visceral fat causes decreases in adiponectin. Lowered adiponectin along with increased TNF-alpha, free fatty acids and resistin causes more insulin in the blood (hyperinsulinemia) which then also increases tumor development (cancer).

The last ones are glucocorticoids, which are a class of steroid hormones. They are prevalent in visceral fat. Glucocorticoids cause weight gain, increased water weight, emotional disturbances, depression and decreased immune responses. More visceral fat leads to more glucocorticoids which leads to more visceral fat - it becomes a vicious cycle.

In conclusion, the focus is belly fat as it defines our shape, releases substances which cause us to eat more and gain more which consequently affects our whole life... This fountain of substances leads to cancer, high blood pressure, diabetes, high cholesterol, blood clots, depression, and more weight. It is believed that this visceral fat starts loading very early in life, but doesn't start detectably upsetting systems until later. In other words, it may not be your fault. It happened before you could choose what to eat. For women, when they hit menopause the problem explodes as they lose some of the protective effects of estrogen. The same lifestyle program before menopause is totally inadequate postmenopausal. Everything must change or it will change.

Foods

Jesus ate the perfect diet for the perfect reasons with the perfect motivation, therefore achieved the perfect results. The deep relationships between food, health, desire, and body functioning has existed ever since man was created. Food was an issue within Eve's disobedience. Certain foods are able to stimulate our reward centers just as a woman's body shape is able to stimulate the man's reward center. By manipulation and chemical alteration, man has created food-type substances that stimulate the reward centers of the brain more than street drugs therefore creating powerful addictions. This is wonderful for corporate sales, but what about the price? Who really knows what they are eating? Jesus was called a glutton but He wasn't. He only ate the same foods as those who were gluttons. His reasons and motivations were different so he wasn't a glutton. With supercharged foods today – how can poor eating be stopped? It isn't gluttony because the quantities aren't the cause of the problem.

Overweight people are usually using more willpower when dieting by going hungry for days.

Animal Foods

Is meat ok? The answer is yes, but we have to be wise about eating it. Yes, becoming a vegetarian reduces risks of cancer, heart disease, diabetes, gout, arthritis and more but not as much as it would seem.[20] Red meat (fresh and processed) contributes to cancer, heart disease, diabetes and high blood pressure.[21] [22] Reducing it would be a wonderful thing. Jesus told a parable of the prodigal son who left his father for the "good life". His life at home was evidently boring to him and the allure of sex, drugs and money overtook him. As usual the effects were short lived. Now impoverished, he returned home repentant and sorrowful. His gracious father ran to him, forgave him and welcomed him with open arms and love. The son was given a great

---

[20] "The long-term health of vegetarians and vegans. - NCBI." 28 Dec. 2018, https://www.ncbi.nlm.nih.gov/pubmed/26707634.
[21] "Red and processed meat intake and cancer risk - NCBI." 16 Oct. 2017, https://www.ncbi.nlm.nih.gov/pubmed/28913916.
[22] "Red and processed meat consumption and mortality ... - NCBI." 6 Jul. 2015, https://www.ncbi.nlm.nih.gov/pubmed/26143683.

celebration with the best part being beef to eat. His brother was furious and blatantly asked his father why he couldn't have beef to eat with his friends. He was the good kid. Beef was used for celebration. Yes, it can be good, but not beef for breakfast, burgers for lunch and roast for dinner everyday. Jesus described it rightfully as a celebratory meal.

So red meat as a celebration is not a problem. The problem is much bigger than meat which is why all of the studies comparing vegetarians with nonvegetarians produce results much less than expected. Just eliminating meat does not necessarily mean healthy. There are many vegetarians that are totally unhealthy. There are many vegans, who will not eat any animal products at all who are thin, but still unhealthy.

The major issue with meat isn't the saturated fat. Saturated just means that the chemical structure is full of hydrogen atoms as opposed to unsaturated which will have one or more double bonds with no hydrogen. Under non-gluttonous quantities all is well.

It isn't the saturated fat that makes fresh red meat so bad. The research is clear that used for celebration (sparingly) red meat is fine, but over use is detrimental to health. In October 2015, the World Health Organization (WHO) published a report concluding that red meat is "probably carcinogenic to humans. Processed meats are truly carcinogenic and listed in the same category (Group 1) as cigarettes and asbestos. The risks may vary but the case for processed meat and cancer is strong. Processed meats are those like bologna, luncheon meat, salami, hot dogs, pepperoni (meaning pizzas), and many frozen meals. We destroy people for smoking but feed them hot dogs and bacon. Foods have "drug like" qualities in changing the way the body works, but drugs are single chemical entities that can be studied and researched as to their effect and still are not fully understood even after 50 years of use. Imagine a food that is composed of many different substances which affects different body mechanisms. The list is endless and the studies will be endless. We are just beginning to see foods as "drug like" so the challenge for science is only a few years old. Nutrition is in its infancy in research, study design and particularly funding.

The conclusion then is to eat fresh red meat if desired, but not with every meal. At 99 cents, it is very hard to resist. McDonald's, Wendy's, Burger King and more have figured out how to send the ground beef smell through the neighborhood. Sweets are better drivers of the hedonistic response to food where we "live to eat" as opposed to trying to "eat to live", but fat is second.[23] Under the right circumstances, almost any food can bring pleasure. Some foods just hit the right spot and give that highly dopaminergic, just good feeling. Inside our brains we have endogenous opiates – yes like heroin. When we eat a burger, it causes the opiates to be released bringing a true "high" like a heroin addict. So when we try to walk away from the McDonald's, it keeps calling us back to where it talks to us and lures us through the drive thru. McDonald's sold 87 million burgers in 2009. We are a nation of burger eaters. That still isn't the main problem though...

---

[23] "Opioids as facilitators of feeding: can any food be rewarding?." 28 Apr. 2011, https://www.ncbi.nlm.nih.gov/pubmed/21536057.

Then we have chicken. Chicken sales are increasing with beef sales decreasing as people switch in an attempt to eat healthier. The issue is not chicken but deep fried chicken. It's finger licking good and has created huge profits around the world particularly in impoverished neighborhoods.

Is God in this? Before Adam Smith wrote The Wealth of Nations he wrote the Theory of Moral Sentiments. Adam Smith is the father of so-called market based economics or the free enterprise system. Rarely has anyone read the Wealth of Nations but definitely hadn't read his first book: The Theory of Moral Sentiments, but the point is that free enterprise without morality leads to chaos – the books were to go together. The free enterprise system in the hands of self-centered individuals hurt people therefore creating an animalistic society where the survival of the fittest mantra rules. For a free market system to work, all people must have equal access to information but with food and medicine –who knows what we are getting? In other words – we can compare soap powders, cars, computers and clothes based upon the information given. How can we compare drugs? How can we compare fried chicken thighs? Who knows how much oil is in them and who knows how much damage it will do to our bodies? Next the free market system is dependent upon ethical businesses that will not knowingly sell products that will harm people. What we see in this new global marketplace is greed and more greed as the world's nutrition is transitioning to super high sugar intakes never before seen in humanity. The new virtual colonization is called the Coca-Colonization where Coca-Cola and the fast food free market universe drives into every community throughout the world reducing prices, changing food taste perceptions, eliminating competition and reducing life expectancy. The United States spent $190 billion in 2012 in farm subsidies mainly to drive down the prices for high fructose corn syrup, trans fats, vegetable oils and corn feed for meat producers which is exactly what fast food restaurants are serving. Less than 1/2 % is going to subsidize fruits and vegetables. Grapes were $4.99 a pound last week. Coke costs less than water! Swinburn and group[24] raised the question: *If the market is failing our children? If prices are no longer indicative of the product's value to society then the market has failed to correct itself.*

Chicken contains omega 6 fatty acids.
So what are omega 6 fatty acids? You have omega 3 and omega 6. Both are unsaturated which means that some bonds are double and without a hydrogen atom, but the omega 6 fatty acids are pro-inflammatory. Omega 3's are anti-inflammatory. When you get a cut on your skin you can watch the inflammatory process begin with pain, redness, immobility (loss of function), swelling and heat: "PRISH". It's the body's way of healing, but when we add pro-inflammatory foods and drugs, it upsets the delicate balance of the immune system leading to more PRISH internally where and when we don't want it. Heart disease rates increase, cancer rates increase, asthma rates increase, diabetes rates increase and more...

---

[24] "The global obesity pandemic: shaped by global drivers and ...." https://www.ncbi.nlm.nih.gov/pubmed/21872749.

Omega 6 fatty acids can be balanced with omega 3 fatty acids which can come from oily fish which we'll discuss later. When Jesus fed people, his choice was fish. The ideal balance of omega 6 to omega 3 is about 1:1 or one meal of fish to one meal of chicken. In the United States our ratio is about 30:1 when we are in overflow of omega 6 – inflammation.

Think of the lungs getting inflamed as you have occurring in this epidemic of asthma. When the immune system is out of balance it overreacts.[25] The inflammatory response begins when an injury occurs or a foreign organism invades the body. The white blood cells go on attack mode to create healing. No drug can do this. It kills the invader and restores the body back to normal where we look brand new. When off balance it keeps attacking even though there is no enemy. Blood vessels get stickier allowing LDL cholesterol to stick to the wall and develop clots faster.[26] Inflammation

[25] "Asthma and obesity: mechanisms and clinical implications ...." 4 Jun. 2015, https://asthmarp.biomedcentral.com/articles/10.1186/s40733-015-0001-7.
[26] "What is cholesterol and how does arteriosclerosis ... - NCBI." 14 Aug. 2013, https://www.ncbi.nlm.nih.gov/books/NBK279327/.

induces tumor creation[27] which may lead to cancer. A healthy immune system should be able to detect cancer cells and eliminate them before causing damage. Cancer is only a cell or cells in the body that divide more than normal. A mole is a cell that divides more than normal, but it stops. A benign tumor is a cell that divided more than normal but stopped. A malignant tumor is a cancer cell that just keeps dividing on and on and doesn't stop. Radiation or chemotherapy can kill the cells, but with the side effect of killing some good cells also. Of course it is better for the body's own immune system to take care of it, but the immune system has to be in balance to be healthy and a proper omega 6 to omega 3 ratio is very important to keep that balance. The research is in the early stages but the chemistry is solid.[28] So the problem with chicken is that most of the fat without the skin is omega 6. Well, when we fry the chicken we dip it in a pot full of refined seed

---

[27] "Interleukin-6 promotes tumorigenesis by altering DNA ...." 7 Jan. 2011, Interleukin-6 promotes tumorigenesis by altering DNA methylation in oral cancer cells..
[28] "Associations of Processed Meat, Unprocessed Red ... - NCBI." 3 Feb. 2020, https://www.ncbi.nlm.nih.gov/pubmed/32011623.

oil which is omega 6![29] [30] [31] Corn oil, heavily subsidized by the government, is the dip of choice and is the number one source of omega 6 fatty acids.

In addition to the omega 6 meat and the omega 6 oil, the feed for chickens which comes mainly from subsidized crops of corn, gives the meat more of an omega 6/omega 3 ratio than they should normally have if grass fed.[32] Watch any video on YouTube about how chickens are processed. The same is true for beef and pork where subsidized corn is used for feed allowing for a poor omega 6/omega 3 ratio in the meat. To get a good idea about inflammation, just think about anti-inflammatory drugs like aspirin or ibuprofen. They inhibit cyclooxygenase or COX. Omega 6 fatty acids produce arachidonic acid which leads to prostaglandins which cause inflammation and pain along with

[29] "Endocrinology - Oxford Academic Journals - Oxford University ...." 8 Jan. 2020, https://academic.oup.com/endo/advance-article/doi/10.1210/endocr/bqz044/5698148.

[30] "Omega-6 fatty acids and inflammation. - PubMed - NCBI - NIH." 22 Mar. 2018, https://www.ncbi.nlm.nih.gov/m/pubmed/29610056/.

[31] "An Increase in the Omega-6/Omega-3 Fatty ...." 2 Mar. 2016, https://www.ncbi.nlm.nih.gov/pmc/articles/PMC4808858/.

[32] "Dietary patterns, subclinical inflammation, incident coronary heart ...." https://www.ncbi.nlm.nih.gov/pubmed/21468094.

thromboxanes which cause clotting in the blood vessels. Yes, there is a controversy as to how much arachidonic acid is produced from omega 6 fatty acids and its actions, but the controversy fails to address the reality that omega 3 fatty acids are so much better than omega 6 fatty acids. And yes, it's a no brainer that omega 6 fatty acids are better than saturated fatty acids from red meat. The level of inflammation that stems from omega 6 intake is in comparison to omega 3 intake. The question is what is the optimal balance.

So if you have a headache or toothache or joint pain or swelling you'll likely take aspirin or ibuprofen. Well since they block COX, the body cannot make prostaglandins and the pain is stopped. Many people take an aspirin a day to prevent blood clotting. By blocking COX the thromboxanes aren't produced therefore less clotting, less chance of stroke, or heart attacks. Why not just decrease the omega 6 intake? Increasing the omega 3 intake can balance it out since omega 3's compete for the same enzymes therefore you get less of an effect from omega 6, but with the American diet at 30:1 omega 6 – there is not much of a fight. KFC, Popeyes and Church's chicken will win every time. Oily fish like salmon or trout is expensive. $8.99 for salmon and $5.99 for trout per pound seems to be the going prices when not on sale. Popeye's just had a 12 piece special for $4.99 let alone the chicken sandwich craze.

This is why diets or prescriptions will never work. Government subsidies create the price issues which create the supply problems where those who can least afford healthier foods end up more diseased but need healthier foods the most. Diets are legalism. Jesus came to free us, not bind us. We bind the devil. We're free to choose, but we need the right information and more importantly we need a relationship with God where the taste of food doesn't control us. An uncontrollable appetite for grease is just lust. Enjoying food is freedom, but being controlled by food is bondage. Jesus said not to worry about what you will eat or what you will wear. Even the Gentiles seek after those things. Jesus is the bread of life. Joy in Him supersedes any pleasure to where nothing else matters. He is that good! To know Him is to love Him is to know Him.

Omega 9 is better than omega 6. Omega 9 is a monounsaturated fatty acid which is a better replacement for omega 6 fats in the diet. Olive oil is a great source. Extra virgin olive oil has been found to contain squalene and phenolic antioxidants which reduce oxidative stress on the body systems which occurs when free radicals or reactive oxygen species (ROS) are out of balance. Free radicals are unpaired electrons that are like poison to cells when out of balance. The body operates through balance as free radicals are normal and can do good work but when out of balance they can cause damage to blood vessels, kill cells, increase inflammation, alter cell DNA, alter fat breakdown and more leading to heart disease, Alzheimer's disease, cancer and more... The body therefore needs a good supply of antioxidants to clean up the over supply of reactive oxygen species (ROS). Well, extra virgin olive oil has antioxidants and also influences the immune system, affects the development of cancer, helps the cells talk to one another (signaling) and the cell's communication with itself through affecting genes. It has a favorable balance of omega 6 and omega 3 fatty acids and a beautiful mixture of the three (3, 6 and 9). Jesus used olive oil to represent His spirit in the parable of the 10 virgins.

Fish

Oily fish is excellent! Salmon, Trout, Mackerel, Sardines, and Herring. They not only are a great source of omega 3 fatty acids, but also contain EPA and DHA. This fish is so powerful, it's like a drug. In fact there is an expensive drug called Lovaza that is just fish oil which is prescribed to lower triglycerides to reduce the risk of heart disease. You can get omega 3 fatty acids from plant sources like flaxseed, but you'd get only a little benefit since the conversion from alpha linoleic acid (ALA) to DHA and EPA is very inefficient. Fish contains omega 3, DHA and EPA therefore conversion is not needed. It is DHA and EPA included that allows oily fish to be so potent. Omega 3 fatty acids have been shown to be effective in cancer, ADHD, depression, retinopathy, hypertriglyceridemia, and atherosclerosis. If taken during pregnancy it has been shown to reduce the risk of obesity and allergies in the offspring. The most interesting study links omega 3 fatty acid intake with reduced damage from heart attacks but its effects are seen best with reduced omega 6 fatty acid use.[33] [34] The pattern stays the same consistently in the advantage of bible guided foods as being the most nutritious and effective. The least natural and most processed foods are consistently the most damaging.[35] Tilapia and Catfish are very inexpensive compared to salmon, but challenging because both are extensively farm raised. The problem with farm raised is that they are fed high omega 6 based diets which again distorts the omega 3/omega 6 ratio.[36] Eating wild is preferable. The challenge is how do we know what we are buying anyway? There is no getting around the establishment of ethical standards that protects the public from damaging foods and provides information concerning

[33] "Prenatal fatty acid status and child adiposity at age 3 y: results ...." https://www.ncbi.nlm.nih.gov/pubmed/21310834.

[34] "Recent findings on the health effects of omega-3 fatty acids ...." 4 Jan. 2013, https://bmcmedicine.biomedcentral.com/articles/10.1186/1741-7015-11-5.

[35] "Ultra-Processed Diets Cause Excess Calorie ... - Cell Press." https://www.cell.com/cell-metabolism/pdf/S1550-4131(19)30248-7.pdf.

[36] "(n-6) and omega-3 (n-3) fatty acids in tilapia and human health." https://www.tandfonline.com/doi/full/10.1080/09637480903140503?scroll=top&needAccess=true.

the health effects of the decisions made at each level from retail to farm.

Fish

Omega-3 fatty acids

(grams per 3-oz. serving)

Herring
1.9–2.0
Salmon (fresh,frozen)
1.1–1.9
Halibut
0.60–1.12
Oysters
0.37–1.14
Crabs
0.27–0.40
Catfish
0.22–0.3
Scallops
0.18–0.34
Canned tuna (light)
0.17–0.24
Cod
0.15–0.24
Lobster
 0.07–0.46
Flounder or sole
0.48
Pollock
0.45

Shrimp
0.29
Clams
0.25
Grouper
0.23
Mahi mahi
0.13

Dairy

Dairy products are interesting. Even with the saturated fat included, disease risks including cancer are not increased. In fact, cardiovascular disease risks can be reduced by using dairy. It doesn't seem to be the calcium and even if it helps, calcium is only part of the picture. The milk proteins, casein and whey, are rich sources of angiotensinogen converting enzyme inhibitory peptides which can lower blood pressure[37] which may be a part of the benefit. The jury is still out as to how, but again God gave us foods to eat that are specifically designed to help us and milk was one of them. The Promised Land was the land of milk and honey!

Science has also become so compartmentalized. The patent laws create incentives to research, manufacture and distribute patentable drugs while whole foods and herbs cannot be patented which means limited profits.

---

[37] "Antihypertensive Peptides from Milk Proteins - NCBI." 19 Jan. 2010, https://www.ncbi.nlm.nih.gov/pmc/articles/PMC3991029/.

Why spend if there is no profit. Billions are then spent to develop single chemical drugs which drive the way we see health and disease. Milk as other nature based foods contribute to health in infinite ways where they all work synergistically together. What would that scientific research look like? It would have to admit the existence of an unknown source who created a special blend, who gave the prescription to prophets so that the people who love Him would follow the prescription by love and trust. Without admitting the existence of God in reasoning, studies on health will always be incomplete (emergent phenomenon). We should start from a fact: milk is good then go from there. A fact: rocks are hard. A fact: the sun is hot. A fact: one plus one equals two. A fact: God loves us. It is wisdom that allows us to use quantitative reasoning and critical thinking to reach conclusions, but to also place in the context of God's power and love. All truth comes from God and by God. The quest of science is truth therefore good science will always lead us in the direction of God. God can only be seen and loved by faith so science can't get us to Him but observing His creation will always illuminate His power to us (Romans 1:20). So it's exciting to see man stumble upon what God has always said in His word. It can be called God's checkmate. Sooner or later man would just find himself unable to sustain life without seeing that the closer we are to God's design for food, the healthier we would be. Also, the closer we are to God's design for why we eat, the healthier we will be. God leads us by love, not rules. Legalism creates imbalances and unnatural desires. It's bondage. We should eat to nourish this temple God designed because we love Him. We love Him and He comes into us to lead and guide us. With Him in us we have power over bondages and any lustful desire. Our tastes change. Our desires change. It is a part of an intimate relationship with Him and it cannot be studied in the lab for we cannot judge anyone's relationship. A questionnaire asking – do you really know Him could never work. If we truly love Him we have power over any enemy including addictions. He doesn't want us to have a dull, boring life but a fruitful, joyous life. There is nothing wrong with pleasure foods like milk! Drink up if you desire...

Grains

The grains (rice, breads, pastas) we choose are much more important than the fats we choose for the body. The differences between white rice and brown rice are enormous. The difference in glycemic index (the amount that the blood sugar rises after eating) is very close, but the difference in insulin response is major. In other words, eating white rice will cause a greater rise in insulin than brown rice. If insulin rises then of course more insulin will lead to more visceral (belly) fat. Remember that free fatty acids released from visceral fat leads to more insulin release which leads to more belly fat so it is a vicious cycle. Refined grains increase insulin which increases belly fat which increases insulin, which adds more belly fat which makes us lethargic, stressful, hypertensive, hyperlipidemic, hyperglycemic, hungrier, and on and on... Published in 2010, Dr. McKeown led a great study at Tufts University in Boston that looked at 2834 Framington Heart Study participants. This is the one that hit the nail on the head. Whole grains reduce belly fat and refined grains increase belly fat.[38] Science is tricky in that things that we've known for many years never hit policy until there are studies to back it up. The problem with that is that it's hard to get financing for studies that won't affect someone's profit. Jethro Kloss, who wrote Back to Eden back in 1939 should be proud of the current scientists. Kloss was just a regular herbal guy but so many of his recommendations have panned to be true. He would rail against white rice and white bread over and over throughout his book. When I first began training academically in nutrition at the Nutrition Institute of Louisiana, one of my instructors would just rip Kloss's book apart. He claimed that it just wasn't science. Kloss was just so convincing and back then, nutrition was basically a fad for "health nuts"... Basically, scientists didn't spend time in nutrition for it was only for counting calories.[39]

---

[38] "Whole- and refined-grain intakes are differentially associated ...." 29 Sep. 2018, https://www.ncbi.nlm.nih.gov/pubmed/20881074.

[39] "Science and Politics of Nutrition: History of ... - NCBI - NIH." 13 Jun. 2018, https://www.ncbi.nlm.nih.gov/pmc/articles/PMC5998735/.

All foods were thought to be equal and therefore until recently they believed there were no bad foods. Kloss was onto something back in 1939 and truly ahead of his time. Without science or the bible backing him up, he fell into fool's territory in so many areas.

Attempting to argue naturalism from purely a scientific perspective is impossible but the bible contains all truth and therefore is stronger than science. The Creator is greater than the creation. Good science will agree with the bible or leave us with questions to ask Jesus when we get to heaven, but we still believe the bible. The big questions in life are too big for science such as who were the dinosaurs? Did God design evolution? Science answers "what" questions and faith answers "why" questions. People need both questions answered and in nutrition, science needs stronger proof. The proof needed to remove soda pop from the market would need to be substantial. Evolutionary biologists use much less rigor to claim we evolved randomly and not by a fine tuned design. Sure, their work is scientific but in medicine the proof has to be much stronger. With the same assurances that are used to advance many theories of the world's origins billions of years ago, we would end up wiping out whole classes of drugs, eliminating most surgeries and wouldn't eat any food at all. Even though science points to a fine tuned universe fine tuned by a creator, some scientists are proposing a theory of multiple universes just to ignore truth. It's called insanity.

In any event though now, science has made great progress in the last 10 years in understanding what naturalists have been saying for centuries. Why did it take so long? How could we have thought we could consume ultra processed food and the body would accept it?[40] Why would we think that the body is so simplistic to accept partially hydrogenated oils and refined grains and trans fats and other creations of laboratories and/or significant destruction of food stuffs?[41] It would just stand to reason that this delicate, complex physical specimen of a body would require only high grade fuel. We only put 93 octane into the

---

[40] "Ultra-Processed Diets Cause Excess Calorie … - Cell Press." https://www.cell.com/cell-metabolism/pdf/S1550-4131(19)30248-7.pdf.

[41] "Association of Low-Carbohydrate and Low-Fat Diets … - NCBI." https://www.ncbi.nlm.nih.gov/pubmed/31961383.

best cars but we thought we could gulp sodas daily and the human machine would work just peachy. Nuts! But that is what science told us. Science is good at small questions but has trouble with big issues like value, integrity, purpose, natural, good, wholesome, etc... It cannot quantify love, peace or joy. God made us and foods to consume but eliminating the God perspective leaves us with only observation. The studies that really highlight "cause and effect" can't exist since we'll never truly understand the synergistic complexity of natural foods or even more so, the human system. This is only a job for God☺.

There is no better illustration than with grains. Removal of the wheat from the chaff is necessary. *Luke 3:15-17 NKJV Now as the people were in expectation, and all reasoned in their hearts about John, whether he was the Christ or not, John answered, saying to all, "I indeed baptize you with water; but One mightier than I is coming, whose sandal strap I am not worthy to loose. He will baptize you with the Holy Spirit and fire. His winnowing fan is in His hand, and He will*

*thoroughly clean out His threshing floor, and gather
the wheat into His barn; but the chaff He will burn
with unquenchable fire."*

John uses wheat as an illustration of a man with a God
centered spirit and the chaff as waste product as a man
whose spirit is self centered. On the threshing floor an
ox (who you should not muzzle – Deuteronomy 25:4) or
other animal walks around and around pulling a
threshing sled (Amos 3:1) which violently broke the
chaff from the grain. The winnowing fan is fanned
allowing the light weight chaff to be blown in the wind
and then burned in the fire while the heavier wheat
containing the bran, germ and endosperm falls to the
threshing floor to be picked up and used. The bad must
be removed from the good, but man has taken the good
along with the bad. Today man uses big combine
machines to harvest the wheat, thresh the wheat and
separate the chaff all in one operation. It is then
brought to a mill to separate the valuable bran and the
germ from the endosperm.

The bran and germ are highly nourishing to the body but the bran is hard and the germ becomes rancid quickly. The bran decreases insulin levels[42] inhibits prostate cancer progression, decreasing visceral adiposity (belly fat),[43] reduces the incidence of large colorectal adenomas,[44] decreases constipation, plus reduces plasma total cholesterol concentrations, triglyceride concentrations, very-low-density lipoprotein cholesterol concentrations, and improves glycemic (blood sugar) control[45] and more...

---

[42] "Rye whole grain and bran intake compared with refined wheat ...." 27 Oct. 2010, https://www.ncbi.nlm.nih.gov/pubmed/2098065

[43] "Whole- and refined-grain intakes are differentially associated ...." 29 Sep. 2018, https://www.ncbi.nlm.nih.gov/pubmed/20881074.

[44] "Wheat bran fiber and development of adenomatous polyps ...." https://www.ncbi.nlm.nih.gov/pubmed/10089114.

[45] "Beneficial effects of high dietary fiber intake in patients with ...." https://www.ncbi.nlm.nih.gov/pubmed/10805824.

Bran and Cholesterol

If we looked at bran as a drug it would be a blockbuster. Oat bran (soluble fiber) can lower cholesterol by 10-15% which is a tad less than some of the statin cholesterol drugs (Pravastatin @ 17%), but with none of the side effects. Oat bran works by inhibiting the synthesis (creation) of cholesterol.[46] Statins also work by inhibiting cholesterol synthesis. It inhibits HMG-CoA reductase which is an enzyme needed to create cholesterol. Oat bran also reduces the absorption of cholesterol in the small intestine by binding to bile acids (made from cholesterol to help the digestion of fat). The majority of cholesterol is used to make bile acids so if you bind and eliminate bile acids then more cholesterol is used to create bile acids, thus lowering cholesterol levels in the body leading to less cholesterol laden clots therefore less heart attacks and strokes. Another class of drugs called bile acid sequestrants (Questran) work that way also. A drug called Zetia

---

[46] "Beneficial effects of high dietary fiber intake in patients with ...." https://www.ncbi.nlm.nih.gov/pubmed/10805824.

(ezetimibe) inhibits the absorption using a different method by directly targeting a sterol transporter, NPC1L1 in the small intestine therefore locking the door so cholesterol can't get into the body. With 30 million people taking statins the implications are enormous. A Canadian researcher found that using a diet portfolio of cholesterol lowering foods reduced LDL cholesterol by 20% for those who stayed with it. Like a stock portfolio of great stocks, this diet portfolio consisted of great foods, such as of course oat bran breads and cereals, oatmeal, brown rice and vegetables. They also added almonds (high in omega 9 and some omega 3 fatty acids) which reduce cholesterol levels. Lastly they added plant sterol enriched margarine (Benecol or Take Control) instead of regular margarine and butter. These products are actually chemically created plant sterols that do lower LDL cholesterol, but have been shown to possibly induce negative cardiovascular effects. In any event, 20% is a very big reduction in LDL that is comparable to that of some of the statins, again without the damaging side effects. Simvastatin 80 mg was just the subject of warnings by the FDA because of the muscle weakness side effects. Rare but severe cases include renal failure and death. Muscle weakness actually persists after stopping the drugs in a third of patients. 87% of patients who told their doctor about the side effects were ignored by their doctor.[47] We'll discuss much more on statins later.

[47] "An efficacy trial of an electronic health record-based ... - NCBI." 2 Jul. 2016, https://www.ncbi.nlm.nih.gov/pmc/articles/PMC5300020/.

The Gut

The effects of whole grains on the gut microbiota (bacteria of the intestines) may be the most important. This is where wheat bran and other insoluble fibers truly become stars. Antibiotics have possibly been the cause of the destruction of the balance of bacteria in our intestine.[48] These trillions of bacteria (10^{14} - more than the number of cells in the human body) are a powerful microbial ecosystem that regulates the amount of food that we take in from the diet, our energy balance and fat storage.

Each part of the digestive tract contains bacteria and viruses with the colon being the largest repository. When babies are born their digestive tract is virtually sterile except for small amounts that may come from amniotic fluid. As a child begins to feed, the bacteria develop rapidly which is a perfectly normal process. The result is called normobiosis of the gut where all of the microorganisms are completely in balance. The focus is

---

[48] "Disruption of the Gut Ecosystem by Antibiotics - NCBI." 29 Nov. 2017, https://www.ncbi.nlm.nih.gov/pmc/articles/PMC5725362/.

currently on the bacteria and fungi with viruses present also. Women understand quite well that when on antibiotics, they many times develop vaginal yeast infections. It's the same principal in the colon where if you kill off the good bacteria, the fungi overgrow. It's a balance.

The first thing that these bacteria do is affect the immune system of the body. Proper balance of the bacteria is essential for a healthy immune system which stands to reason that if there are 10 times more bacteria than human cells, the body is outnumbered therefore the bacteria must be kept in check. The immune system is the warrior system of the body that identifies, then goes on the attack whenever some enemy enters the body. It can kill them, engulf and chew them or neutralize them. When the microbiota of the gut is out of balance, they affect inflammatory mediators within the body: eicosanoids and steroids which in turn affect the body's immune function. Remember the eicosanoids from the discussion on omega 6 and omega 3 fats? The immune system affects every function in the body and is affected by all the things that the body comes in contact with. It is particularly affected by mood, excitement, joy, sadness, fitness, nutrition and more... It truly is a barometer to the body.

So obviously antibiotics play a major role in the gut. Antibiotics kill bacteria. The big question for now though is what about the antibiotics given to livestock? Pigs, cows and chickens were given antibiotics (added to their feed) to make them fatter quicker, not just to cure disease from around the 1940's to 2017. Antibiotics use is still regulated voluntarily to allow prophylactic use with veterinarian oversight but growth promotion has been banned.[49] Will the use of antibiotics drop considerably? Why would veterinarians be more responsible than physicians and pharmacists? They all have huge incentives. The question being asked is only of antibiotic resistance, but now we're looking at obesity, diabetes, heart disease, cancer, depression, psychosis, Alzheimer's, ADHD and more so the implications are much, much bigger...

---

[49] "Does the use of antibiotics in food animals pose a risk to human." https://www.ncbi.nlm.nih.gov/pubmed/14657094.

We're on a new frontier of science here with big financial interests to fight but the stakes are high and the benefits are enormous. One thing is certain though in that as we better understand the gut, its implications for antibiotic use becomes more and more apparent. Just like as the steel roller mill was invented in the 1870's with major implications for human health, we see antibiotics, which were placed in use in 1944 now becoming more important in our understanding of human health and disease. 4500 years ago Egyptian records mention antimicrobials with Nubians even using tetracycline 1600 years ago in a low alcoholic grain cereal. The use of antibiotics now has exploded to where the average child gets 10 – 20 prescriptions of antibiotics by 18 years of age. 60% of adults get antibiotics for colds and flu which are caused by viruses. A recent study of over 5000 children showed significant BMI increases in children who were repeatedly exposed to antibiotics.[50] The

---

[50] "Association of Repeated Antibiotic Exposure Up to Age 4 ...." 22 Jan. 2020, https://jamanetwork.com/journals/jamanetworkopen/fullarticle/2759122.

information/social media age floods the world with information but basic science is complex. Chemistry is a challenging subject. Physics is challenging. Biology is more than applied chemistry and physics. Medical care is more than applied biology. Life is more than applied medical care.

Marketers are jamming in new products and marketing strategies to promote "organic" , "antibiotic free", and a myriad of other slogans to give an aura of health. The problem is that there's no proof that any of it will make a difference. If the cow we ate didn't receive antibiotics then does it mean that the cow never had an imbalance of microorganisms? What's worse? If one of my children were never given antibiotics and the others were, does that mean that the antibiotic free child was healthier? The real question is who is cared for? Care may include antibiotics or may not. It may include inorganic or organic pesticides or it may not. We need decision makers who primarily care and are willing to treat people the way they would like to be treated. They will then continually educate themselves to the best practices available because they have a heart. Grocery stores and medical facilities are battle grounds for truth. The grocers and restaurateurs aren't challenged but the medical community is attacked not to reduce medications and procedures but to give medicines and procedures. People want cures and want them immediately and love antibiotics therefore be kind to the physicians because patients demand prescriptions. If the doctor doesn't give one, they may lose the patient quickly or get sued. All day long I'm telling patients to drink water for their cold (productive cough and mucous congestion), but they want a drug. Water works better, but if they really want a drug, guaifenesin is the least harmful as opposed to pseudoephedrine or phenylephrine which acts like speed on the brain and heart. A productive cough is productive to get the mucus out – not to let it stay in. It just needs to be thinned out with water. We are a drug taking society believing not in healthcare but a nanny system that will solve our every problem. The medical system becomes a god. Better knowledge about antibiotics doesn't help either[51] which is indicative of medical worship. Even when people knew better they still desired antibiotics – the more educated patients just completed the therapy - they took all of the pills until finished! The explosion in microbiome research has brought a new perspective on how the body works and its power and sensitivity. Those trillions of living organisms inside of us affect us in a way that is reshaping nutrition, pharmacy, medicine and ultimately life itself. They are amazing.

The next thing that they do is decide which and how much food that the body takes in. In other words: you can spend all the time you want deciding what to eat, but the trillions of bacteria in your intestines truly decide what you eat. They keep what they want and eliminate the rest. Not only that, they decide how much belly fat to give you from the food you eat. These guys are amazing... When you go to Saks 5th Avenue to try on that dress and it doesn't fit – blame the guys in your intestines. A 42% increase in food intake was observed

---

[51] "Animations designed to raise patient awareness of prudent ...." 6 Dec. 2017, https://www.ncbi.nlm.nih.gov/pmc/articles/PMC5718068/.

in one study along with increases in triglycerides, glucose and insulin. The microbes increase the uptake of mono and polysaccharides (sugars) but also stimulate two enzymes that increase fat storage: ChREBP and perhaps SREBP-1. The microbes operate another way also to increase triglyceride storage by suppressing (fasting induced adipose factor) Fiaf which is a substance produced in fat which leads to the breakdown of fat to keep a balance. The microbes block Fiaf which increases lipoprotein lipase (LPL) which is a substance that increases triglyceride storage.[52] These guys are super smart...

It is postulated that the substance that causes all of this is the part of the gram negative bacteria called the endotoxin which secretes lipopolysaccharide (LPL). When they get out of balance in the gut, it's called endotoxemia. It has been found that this LPL is what causes insulin resistance and adds to body weight gain. LPL is promoted by a high fat diet. We already stated

---

[52] "The gut microbiota as an environmental factor that regulates ...." https://www.ncbi.nlm.nih.gov/pubmed/15505215.

how belly fat shoots out all of the fiery substances to cause inflammation but LPL is postulated to be the one which keeps this fountain flowing.

A high refined carbohydrate/high fat diet causes changes in the gut microbial composition in hours. These guys multiply so fast that it doesn't take long for their composition to be totally changed – trillions of them. In a few days you can have a complete makeover for it is the diet that dominates the decision on which microbes reproduce and which ones do not, for they feed upon this food to continually create a balance.[53] So they decide what we actually bring into the body, but we decide who they are. They can be hired or fired to give us the health we are entitled to.

So the microbial population of the gut does many, many things. In addition to regulating fat storage, glucose levels, and inflammatory responses – they also produce short chain fatty acids which stimulate the release of

---

[53] "The effect of diet on the human gut microbiome: a ... - NCBI - NIH." https://www.ncbi.nlm.nih.gov/pubmed/20368178.

leptin which regulates appetite.[54] This is fascinating and more research is needed, but the results so far only validate what has already been observed and that is, eating Jesus based foods leads to a healthier life. Currently probiotics are all the rage – giving people bacteria in a pill to replace the bacterial imbalances. Sure on antibiotics it may make sense, but people are really looking for a pill again to solve their problems. The last point to make here about the gut microbial world is that it is so huge and complex and so new that it will truly be years before we truly have an understanding of the symbiotic relationship between man, microorganisms, food and the outside environment. What we see now is that we are totally related to everything else. We are related to the people around us, the food we eat, the air we breathe, and the God we serve. God designed all in such a balance that faith in Him cannot help but increase as we see His works. This is no accident! So eat whole grains with the

---

[54] "Gut microbiome, obesity, and metabolic dysfunction. - NCBI." https://www.ncbi.nlm.nih.gov/pubmed/21633181.

bran intact – eat fruits and vegetables, eat beans, drink water. Love God, love life... QSS!

Breads

Jesus said: I am the bread of life!

The ancient Egyptians baked fermented bread 4000 years ago, using old dough as leaven to add to the new dough which allows the bread to rise. With that said of course whole wheat bread is best, but most whole wheat breads are full of sugar. Each slice of bread has roughly the same amount of sugar as a Chips Ahoy cookie. White breads are enriched with iron and the B vitamins--niacin, thiamin, riboflavin, and folic acid. When the steel roller mill destroyed the bran and took the germ out of the grain, people started getting pellagra (niacin deficiency) and beriberi (thiamine deficiency). According to the Flour Fortification Initiative: *much of wheat's nutritional value is lost as the wheat is milled, and this loss can easily be restored or increased through fortification. All the food subsequently made with fortified flour boosts the consumer's intake of those nutrients without requiring*

a change in their behavior.[55] It goes on to say:
Currently 60 countries have legislation that requires
fortification of at least one type of wheat flour with at
least iron and/or folic acid. Worldwide, 30 percent of
the flour from large roller mills is fortified, and the
remaining 70 percent represents a tremendous
potential to improve the lives of millions of people.

The question is why are we removing the germ and bran anyway? As we said beginning in about 1870 with the invention of the steel roller mill, the bran was able to be removed. Prior to that removing the bran without the germ made the flour rancid quickly and before the steel mill there was no easy way to remove the germ except by sifting and sifting by hand where only the rich, refined people could afford it.

Today Sylvester Graham (1794-1851) is known for crackers named after him (graham crackers), but Sylvester Graham was a leading whole grain advocate in his day. His father and grandfather were Calvinist

---

[55] "Eradicating dangerous bacteria may cause ... - EurekAlert!." 24 Aug. 2011,
https://www.eurekalert.org/pub_releases/2011-08/nlmc-edb082211.php.

ministers while he became a Presbyterian minister developing the Graham System which included legalistic vegetarianism, hard mattresses, fruits and vegetables, abstinence from alcohol, masturbation, spices, sugars and all pleasures. Even before the steel roller mill was invented, Graham railed against sifted, refined grains that removed the nutrients from flour and advocated for a grain that was ground, but still left the bran and germ. He upset the doctors, bakers, butchers, tobacco growers, brewers, and saloon keepers which saw their profits decrease as he and his followers (The Grahamites) pushed their cause. He had zeal, but wasn't according to knowledge as he went past the bible and science.

You can find graham flour in some super markets today where that contribution to health was far ahead of his time. The problem is that you can rarely find any bread that is 100% whole wheat without sugar. Even the wheat has had the bran and germ removed in the milling process then added back to the refined flour to make a "put together" wheat flour. The bran has been milled so finely that the effectiveness in the gut has to be questioned. You can find whole wheat bread with a texture as soft as white bread. The germ is placed back, but what about the oil that becomes rancid after exposure to air? The oil is a great source of vitamin E. The addition of wheat germ to a diet resulted in a 7 fold increase in vitamin E content in plasma. As cardiovascular disease is understood to be largely a disease of the endothelial lining of the vessel wall, vitamin E is a powerful antioxidant which decreases the damage caused by reactive oxygen species on lipid (fat) membranes of the wall. After a meal the blood vessels experience oxidative stress evidenced by increases in inflammation, adhesion and endothelial dysfunction which are three factors primarily leading to plaque formation.[56] Vitamin E reduces the oxidative stress thereby keeping the blood vessels clear. Wheat germ is a great source of vitamin E in addition to containing niacin and thiamine as stated earlier. The fermented extract of wheat germ (FWGE) has antiproliferative (growth stopping) effects killing cancer cells through

---

[56] "Postprandial lipid oxidation and cardiovascular disease risk ...."
https://link.springer.com/article/10.1007/s11883-004-0089-3.

causing their death (apoptosis). It is shown to have significant effects in melanoma and colon cancer with data so far justifying its use.[57] It is easy to see why whole grains are disease protectors while refined grains are disease causers. One is a cure and the other is a poison - opps. Scientists cannot use such terms, but clearly the data expresses the dangers and zero nutritional value of refined grains. The intake of empty calories that promote disease progression can only be called a threat to the human system – toxin.

One of the best breads that we find on the market today can be found in the freezer: sprouted wheat bread. The grain is not milled into flour, but the grain is moistened with water allowing the wheat seed to grow (germinate). The sprouted seeds are then ground and made into dough, baked then frozen and transported. It can last out of the freezer for 5 days, but of course after that it can become rancid since the germ oils are included and not milled out. Sprouting can also be a

---

[57] "Fermented wheat germ extract - Nutrition Journal - BioMed ...."
5 Sep. 2011,
https://nutritionj.biomedcentral.com/articles/10.1186/1475-2891-10-89.

source of E. coli or salmonella poisoning if proper agricultural and preparation techniques are not used as sprouting seeds also provides a rich medium for bacterial growth. There is a company from California that sells it as Ezekiel 4:9 bread:

Take thou also unto thee wheat, and barley, and beans, and lentils, and millet, and fitches, and put them in one vessel, and make thee bread thereof, according to the number of the days that thou shalt lie upon thy side, three hundred and ninety days shalt thou eat thereof.

The scripture doesn't actually call for sprouting it, but the concept is nice. The same can be done for grinding wheat using the Graham technique (also called unbolted wheat flour), where the germ and the bran are included. Just look for graham flour at the store. The courser the flour, the better it should be nutritionally. When the wheat is ground using stones instead of steel, the temperature can be kept low preventing destruction of the germ. Hodgson Mills calls it cold grinding. More studies are needed to quantify the nutritional value of finer wheat which is basically a pulverized grain.

The Corruption of Bran

The question for the finer wheat is; how can it stay fresh without the germ becoming rancid? Called all over and could not find anyone to give the answer. We had a television program called Health Issues and asked Dr. Finley, a food scientist with a degree in biochemistry to tell the story. He went on to say that when he worked for a major food manufacturer, a young executive brought in a new whole-wheat product to introduce to the other executives. It was wrapped in cellophane. He opened it and the smell was horrible. The other executives told him to get it out of there. The problem was that the germ had become rancid. Well that is what happens with whole-wheat flour, but it is always wrapped in paper so the smell dissipates. By the time it gets to the shelves at the grocery store, all smells fine, but the germ oxidized anyway. Cellophane holds the odor, but paper lets it out. Better if possible to buy freshly ground flour or grind it yourself. If necessary, the rancidity may be ok since it is better than refined flour but this needs to be studied.

Since we are now looking at the germ and bran clinically and medicinally, it is of utmost importance that these studies be funded and properly performed as our health is dependent upon the answers... Thanks Dr. Finley...

So what do we buy then? Well it should be 100% whole wheat without any added sugar, high fructose corn syrup, brown sugar, etc... Honey is fine, but rarely will you find any honey wheat without added sugars. We'll discuss sugars later, but most breads as we stated are like a cookie. The nutrition label was pretty worthless until in 2020, a Michelle Obama initiative led to listing the amount of added sugars on the label. Sodium content was the only true useful item where breads are usually low in sodium. The ingredient list is the key for bread and everything else in the grocery store. The way the FDA has criminalized this is still to allow any item that is 51% or more whole wheat to be called whole wheat. So the first item will be whole wheat, but the second item may be sugar and the third can be refined wheat. It is also called enriched wheat which is just the endosperm with folic acid, niacin, thiamine and iron added back in – no germ or bran. When most people see enriched wheat it sounds like it is healthy, but truly it isn't.

A big item now is 12 grain and 15 grain bread. Well of course, they use wheat but there are many other grains that can be possibly added.

A few other grains:

Amaranth –

It is actually a pseudo-grain, but historically it has been used as a cereal grain. Domesticated 6000 to 8000 years ago it was a favorite food of the Aztecs, called a grain of their gods. It was mixed with honey and shaped into deities to be eaten as communion in their pagan religious services. The Christians banned it in an attempt to purge pagan religious worship in their effort to force Christianity on the native peoples. Obviously they were pseudo Christians banning a pseudo grain.

Amaranth has been shown to lower cholesterol similarly to whole oats and is gluten free so since a pseudo cereal – it can be used for those allergic to cereal grains. The seeds can be popped like popcorn, flaked like oatmeal, or ground into flour for use in breads, noodles, pancakes, cereals, or other flour-based products. The leaves of the plant can also be eaten like a vegetable. It is high in protein, fiber, lysine (possibly decreases anxiety), magnesium (muscle and nerve function), calcium (stronger bones/decreases blood pressure), and squalene (potential chemoprotective, immunostimulant(ga2)). It has more calcium (307mg per cup) than spinach or milk. Amaranth is a powerful food that should be available as interest grows.

Barley

Deuteronomy 8:8 describes the promised land: *A land of wheat, and barley, and vines, and fig trees, and pomegranates; a land of olive oil, and honey...*

Barley is an amazing grain. Specifically beta glucan contained within the cell walls of barley (and oats) has been shown to positively affect the immune system. Drug companies are currently developing drugs that contain beta glucan to fight cancer and infections. Barley beta glucan has been shown to reduce the glycemic response (lowering glucose levels in blood) but more importantly it reduces the insulin response even more so. Subjects given barley beta glucan had a lower response to a sugar load (OGTT) and had greater sensitivity to insulin. Less insulin = less visceral fat. Barley contains soluble fiber which of course lowers cholesterol also. As powerful as barley is, 51% is used for animal feed, 3% for seeds and 44% for beer production. Only 2% is used for human food. There are significant similarities between oats and barley in terms of soluble fiber and beta glucan content. Barley actually contains more fiber and selenium and is more flavorful to many...

Hard Red Winter Wheat (HRW) is grown in the winter and can withstand very cold temperatures as low as -15 degrees F. HRW along with Hard Red Spring and Soft Red Winter Wheat account 80% of wheat grown in the US with Hard White, Soft White and Durum rounding out the rest.

In 1924 medical doctor Charles Edward Shell wrote to the British Medical Journal,

When the steel "roller flour mill" were introduced into this country from America a vital injury was inflicted on our national well-being....[the flour] lacks the proteins, fat, vitamins, and mineral constituents present in the original grain, providing only an emasculated substitute which is not merely inefficient, but also directly harmful. For a dietary overloaded with starchy material produces fermentation and flatulence : it favours the development of an abundant intestinal flora embarrassing to the digestive economy, burdensome to the gastrointestinal organs, and favourable to the free development and increased virulence of such pathogenic microbes as may obtain access to the intestinal tract.

Society denigrates with children being the most affected. Any trip to the grocery store will highlight the amount of foods that are grain based and only 1% of Americans eat the recommended amount of whole grains. 20% do not eat any whole grains. This study counted corn chips and popcorn as whole grains though. It did not adjust for the oils, butter or salt in the mix. The largest portion (45%) came from cold breakfast cereals where the majority is loaded with sugar like Frosted Mini Wheat or Honey Nut Cheerios.

Vegetables/Fruits

Below is a clinical controlled trial published 2800 years in the Journal of God:

10 Day Vegan Diet vs. Standard Kings Diet in Healthy Boys

"During the third year of King Jehoiakim's reign in Judah, King Nebuchadnezzar of Babylon came to Jerusalem and besieged it. The Lord gave him victory over King Jehoiakim of Judah and permitted him to take some of the sacred objects from the Temple of God. So Nebuchadnezzar took them back to the land of Babylonia and placed them in the treasure-house of his god. Then the king ordered Ashpenaz, his chief of staff, to bring to the palace some of the young men of Judah's royal family and other noble families, who had been brought to Babylon as captives. "Select only strong, healthy, and good-looking young men," he said. "Make sure they are well versed in every branch of learning, are gifted with knowledge and good judgment, and are suited to serve in the royal palace. Train these young men in the language and literature of Babylon." The king assigned them a daily ration of food and wine from his own kitchens. They were to be trained for three years, and then they would enter the royal service. Daniel, Hananiah, Mishael, and Azariah were four of the young men chosen, all from the tribe of Judah. The chief of staff renamed them with these Babylonian names: Daniel was called Belteshazzar. Hananiah was called Shadrach. Mishael was called Meshach. Azariah was called Abednego. But Daniel was determined not to defile himself by eating the food and wine given to them by the king. He asked the chief of staff for permission not to eat these unacceptable foods. Now God had given the chief of staff both respect and affection for Daniel. But he responded, "I am afraid of my lord the king, who has ordered that you eat this food and wine. If you become pale and thin compared to the other youths your age, I am afraid the king will have me beheaded." Daniel spoke with the attendant who had been appointed by the chief of staff to look after Daniel, Hananiah, Mishael, and Azariah. "Please test us for ten days on a diet of vegetables and water," Daniel said. "At the end of the ten days, see how we look compared to the other young men who are eating the king's food. Then make your decision in light of what you see." The attendant agreed to Daniel's suggestion and tested them for ten days. At the end of the ten days, Daniel and his three friends looked healthier and better nourished than the young men who had been eating the food assigned by the king. So after that, the attendant fed them only vegetables instead of the food and wine provided for the others." Daniel 1:1-16 NLT Conclusion:This controlled clinical trial found the vegan diet to be superior to the king's diet. At the end of 10 days the vegan diet produced healthier looking and better nourished men. All were healthy to begin with but the health was enhanced by the vegan diet. The King James Version calls it a pulse diet which would imply a variety of beans — kidney, fava, lima, cannellini, pinto, baked, garbanzo, runner, soy, peanuts, lentils, green peas, and black-eyed peas and more. The Hebrew word used is zeroa which most other Bibles translate as a vegetable instead of pulse. This vegetable diet would include grains also.

All of the men were Jewish so pork was not part of their basic diets prior to captivity but may have been a part of the kings diet which consisted of an abundance of meat. A vegan diet is superior to a daily predominantly meat diet.

It has taken 2800 years for nutrition science to duplicate this study. Just recently the world health organization published their warnings on large red meat consumption. These facts are still being energetically challenged by pro-meat advocates. They push paleo and ketogenic diets for lifestyle changes. Ketogenic diets which severely restrict carbohydrates and switch the body to use ketones as the source of energy may be useful in epilepsy and some metabolic diseases short term but for lifestyle changes, vegetable based diets are superior and can still be low carb.

The Bible and the consensus of current research agrees in the value of vegetables. Plants were the basis of almost all medicines until recently. They work synergistically, which means one plus one may equal 1000. In my 25 years of teaching herbal medicine, what fascinates me most is synergism. To observe how various substances in plants work together to produce its medicinal effects and be a food also is amazing. Yes, research has not been able to produce many herbal remedies for consumer use but this is only because of funding. To say herbs have no value would be false since considerable time and energy is spent on discussing herb side effects and drug herb interactions. If they were innocuous they wouldn't have any side effects. Plants can have a powerful effect on the body. The issue will always be matching the effects with the diseases and validating the data through research. Smith described it best when discussing Ginkgo Biloba whose roasted seeds are eaten as a vegetable in many Asian countries. He stated: as opposed to pharmacologically manufactured or synthetic drugs, which provide a single target for a single receptor as the mechanism of action, "EGb 761 is able to up- or down-regulate signaling pathways, gene transcription, cellular metabolism, etc., and thus assist in the regulation of the general physiological status of the cell and/or organism in response to stressors posed by both intracellular and extracellular conditions. Presumably, this is one of the biggest advantages of using natural products for the prevention and treatment of infirmity, as well as the maintenance -of health in an organism"Wonderfully described by Smith et al. in 2004.[58] Smith described the true advantage of not only herbs but vegetables, fruits and grains themselves as a process that man could not replicate or ever fully understand. It's like the difference between a musician playing the same note over and over as opposed to an orchestra playing a wonderful complex piece of music. There is a big conductor named God who has designed the music of life to harmoniously and rhythmically work together. Nutrition as a science is very new and impossible to separate from belief systems. Research in nutrition is inherently biased based upon the researcher's diet which is a subset of his/her belief system. Instead of ignoring the biases and beliefs, science must disclose and study to allow positive, helpful nutrition to be available to the public across cultures. It will never reach 100% accuracy and neither

---

[58] "Studies on molecular mechanisms of Ginkgo ... - NCBI - NIH." https://www.ncbi.nlm.nih.gov/pubmed/14740187/.

does any other medical research but it would be a major step forward. Just honest disclosure will advance our knowledge. Particularly in nutrition, the body's interplay with the mind which reacts to its environment leading to epigenetic changes, evidenced by telomere length affecting each cell of the body along with affecting the microbiome of the gut, vagina, semen and more, all create a system so advanced that it is truly beyond man's ability to ever fully comprehend. For science to advance in nutrition it must acknowledge the unknown, disclose beliefs and focus on its true role of establishing facts. Truths are within belief systems. Like on Dragnet: science should just stick to the facts....

Onions are amazing. Great cooks know how to use them but they are a powerful medicine. They contain alliins, fructosans, saccharose, flavonoids, and steroid saponins. They have antimicrobial and antifungal properties. Onions inhibit platelet aggregation, have hypoglycemic, diuretic, antihyperlipidemic and anticholesterolemic actions. They also cause reduced bronchial secretions.

Vegetables have medicinal properties but are not single target entities. We don't eat just one vegetable. We eat a variety of foods which when blended together work synergistically to produce an effect. A vegetable will work on multiple targets of the body unlike synthetic drugs which focus on a single target of the body. Pharmacologists create a single chemical to attack a single target. God made vegetables to have numerous constituents that exert effects on multiple areas of the body with varying rates and degrees. Again it's like music. It's a full band as opposed to a single monotone note annoyingly played repeatedly. Synthetic drugs are sometimes a necessary evil to rebalance the body. If your blood pressure is 220/120 then vegetables are not your answer. You'll die. You need synthetic medicines that target specific organ systems and processes in the body to immediately lower your pressure. If your blood sugar is 700mg/dl then you need insulin immediately injected under your skin to cause the sugar in your bloodstream which is at toxic levels to get into your cells to be used as energy or be converted to fat for storage particularly around the belly. Yes it will lead to weight gain and belly fat over a very short time but you have no choice. You'll die. Our medical system is addicted to drugs because we are addicted to sugar and refined carbohydrates. The hypoglycemic action of onions would have no effect on a blood sugar of 700mg/dl. I believe in miracles but that's foolish. Prayer works and God can use river water or mud but the power wouldn't be in the mud or the onion but God. That's how Jesus operated. He raised the dead and healed the sick but Luke the physician kept his job before, during and after Jesus's three year ministry. We must meet the need not based upon anything but proven and tested methods. If it is a drug then so be it. Herbal medicine is a concentrated use of a food for a disorder of the body. Synthetic drugs can also be used for a disorder where needed. Processed foods cause most of the disorders so processed medicines are usually the needed treatment to rebalance the body. After that, medicine/foods can keep the body in balance.

Onions are thought to exert their effects by alleviating metabolic dysregulation of free fatty acids, suppressing oxidative stress, up-regulating glucose uptake in peripheral tissues, and/or down-regulating inflammatory gene expression in liver. Each of these mechanisms directly affect visceral fat accumulation and endothelial dysfunction thereby altering the course of cardiovascular disease, diabetes, cancer and more.

Garlic

The National Cancer Institute, part of the National Institutes of Health, does not recommend any dietary supplement for the prevention of cancer, but recognizes garlic as one of several vegetables with potential anticancer properties.

Garlic may act as an HMG-CoA reductase inhibitor which is the same mechanism by which statins exert their effects. It may be a potent inhibitor of hepatic cholesterol synthesis. It reduces oxidative stress, inhibits low-density lipoprotein (LDL) oxidation,[59] has antithrombotic effects, antiplatelet activity, causes smooth muscle relaxation and vasodilation. Garlic also

---

[59] "Suppression of LDL Oxidation by Garlic - Oxford Academic ...." 1 Apr. 2001, https://academic.oup.com/jn/article/131/3/985S/4687061.

seems to have humoral and cellular immunostimulant activity, antimicrobial activity, antidiabetic, and is a hepatoprotectant. It also tastes great.

The list of diseases that garlic may help is long. As with all medicinal foods more research is needed but for the National Institute of Health to validate garlic's potential role in cancer is tremendous. Reducing oxidative stress is an action that has tremendous implications where millions take antioxidants daily to reduce diseases in which the antioxidants themselves may actually cause harm, but increasing garlic seasoning will make a better cook and a healthier family. Ray Charles could see God in this.

What are the best fruits and vegetables...

"The LORD God planted a garden eastward in Eden, and there He put the man whom He had formed. And out of the ground the LORD God made every tree grow that is pleasant to the sight and good for food. Genesis

God gives life. What vegetables and fruits are best to eat. It is a mystery that may never be solved. The Bible doesn't list all foods. Some plants are toxic such as poisonous mushrooms. Science is just recognizing the medicinal value of foods so our science research system is incapable of nutritionally or clinically validating all herbs, vegetables of fruits. We have to review traditional use also for nutritional decisions but clinical use must undergo studies before placing into clinical practice. Very few have been financed sufficiently to place into clinical use what has been used effectively for thousands of years. We must therefore place great value on traditional use, not waiting for research to completely validate. Safety should be the first concern but foods consumed safely and deliciously for generations should be encouraged. Natural is not a good term because there are toxic natural substances.

In April of 2011, the European Union established The European Directive on Traditional Herbal Medicinal

Products. This provided a more structured regulatory framework requiring approval before the selling and marketing of herbs. One of the eligibility criteria was that "the intended use of herbal medicines would only be authorised on the basis of its traditional history and/or the recognised pharmacological properties of the herbal ingredient(s)." Sounds the same as for fruits and vegetables. They have pharmacological value and tradition use should guide policies.

The keto movement is gaining steam and as a response to a sugar driven world it works. The problems are that the pendulum is swinging too much. Sugar and refined carbohydrates are the problem. Good carbs like fruits and vegetables are necessary and medicinal. They can have an unspecified amount of phytonutrients which we learn more about all the time. We know of the health and medicinal benefits of many of the fruits and vegetables but we don't know which substance affects which disease. The USDA only tracks 150 substances anyway. As of August 2019, FooDB recorded the presence of 26,625 distinct biochemicals in food. That number is expected to increase in the near future.[60] These phytochemicals work synergistically so studying one would not give the complete picture. Taking beta carotene may increase the risk of cancer but within a vegetable it is a powerful antioxidant that may help prevent cancer. Again it's like a single horn playing one note or a 100 piece band playing a wonderful piece of music. In this case it is a 26,625 piece band...

Only a tiny fraction of phytochemicals have been studied with hardly any studied in depth. There are unlimited unknowns in fruits and vegetables but what is known is that they prevent disease. They are just beginning to study the nutrigenomic effects of some of the phytochemicals in the bran layer of brown rice. Nutrigenomics is the study of how nutrients affect gene expression. We can see the power of brown rice in metabolic diseases such as diabetes and cardiovascular disease as opposed to white rice. The effects are so much more than insulin response differences and glycemic load variations. Yes we use it as a primary

[60] "The unmapped chemical complexity of our diet | Nature Food." 9 Dec. 2019, https://www.nature.com/articles/s43016-019-0005-1.

mechanism in discussing QSS because people need to somewhat understand what is going on but in no way is it the only or final answer. In fact there are no mechanisms that can fully be explained as new information is revealed regularly as new studies are undertaken. Nutrition is a very complex science. The carbohydrate insulin theory of obesity is a major step in the right direction as opposed to the calorie balance model but neither take into account the myriad of phytochemicals and the unlimited variations in possible effects based upon synergism. The true answer is that we will never know the full power of whole fruits and vegetables. We will never know God's full power either. We will never know the full power by which God fine tuned the universe. One scientist said obtaining a single protein would be the equivalent of a star system of blind men simultaneously solving the rubik's cube. God is the creator and sustainer of all things and He specifically designed foods for us.

Sugars

Free sugar is poison. Sugar alone without a fiber matrix damages the body in any amount. An apple is nutritious but apple juice is damaging. Once we remove the sugar from its fiber it is then a free sugar. Cakes, cookies, juices, smoothies, all contain sugar removed from its fiber through processing.

Sugar is the dominant disease causing substance in the world. Non-communicable diseases have surpassed malnutrition, diarrhea, and infections in developing countries therefore nutrition related diseases top the death list. Sugar is dominant because of the combination of its addictive properties, social acceptability, economic power and its metabolic disease causing properties. It's so much worse than trans fats, processed meats, deep fried foods, refined carbohydrates, marijuana, crack cocaine, alcohol, cigarettes and ecstasy. Satan has a tool in sugar.

Slavery dropped the price of sugar so low that it went from a delight only of the rich to an everyday staple around the world. In the history of mankind there is no other substance that has been able to kill millions of people so effectively with almost no opposition. The few scientists that speak out are not a part of the conversation. The narrative is moderation as if we're talking about red meat. It's like trying to tell a 30 year cigarette smoker to cut back. It's like telling parents to cut back on giving their children dangerous toys that may kill them. It's like telling people to cut back on sex before marriage causing less unwed pregnancies. Moderation...

Sugar is a drug. The damage is not proportional to the amount consumed. Small amounts can cause big damage. A big fallacy people have is when they take a 0.1mg drug and believe it's tiny. Then they take another drug which is 1000mg and believe it is strong. They will also look at pill size. Big pills are strong and little pills are weak. So when every bit of information bombards us overwhelmingly everyday for our entire lives saying sugar is good in moderation how could anyone not expect the death rate to not be so high? Babylon is here. The battle is truly spiritual where the fight must be placed as good versus evil. It was Daniel and the Hebrew boys who were taken captive in Babylon who refused to eat the king's delicacies. They refused to bow down to the golden image and were thrown into the fiery furnace. We need prophets that refuse to bow down and will stand flat footed and speak against this evil. It's not a sin to eat sugar but it's a sin to be addicted, a sin to market it as good knowing it causes addictions, a sin to market to children, a sin to not teach the truth in schools, a sin the not train the health community, a sin for hospitals, pharmacies and dietitians to promote and sell free sugar, a sin for sugar companies to sponsor health and sporting events, a sin for big sugar to finance scientific research twisted to hide their agenda. They are behind the moderation push, and they are behind the move more/eat less slogan, and they are behind the all calories are equal concept. Toys are in sugar cereals, sugar is in baby foods and sugar is sold as the answer to hunger pains. Sugar kills more people than war, gang violence, gun violence, sexual diseases and drug abuse combined. Only mass incarceration is a greater plague on our society but that is another book.

Fructose

Table sugar is composed of fructose and glucose.
Fructose is sweeter. Fructose is metabolized to glucose
in the gut when consumed with fiber such as in fruit but
when consumed as sucrose or high fructose corn syrup
it overloads the gut and is carried to the liver as
fructose.[61] This is where the drama begins. The question
is does free fructose preferentially cause belly fat? Yes it
does because it is separated (freed) from fiber. A good
term to use is "free sugar". Coca Cola and the other big
food companies dispute this fact to claim all calories are
equal.[62] Free fructose is toxic and addictive. Huge sums
of money will be lost if fructose is labeled for what it
does so Big Food has corrupted the science to present a
fructose calorie as equivalent to a broccoli calorie. Since
1995, about $81.7 billion in taxpayer money went to

---

[61] "The Small Intestine Converts Dietary Fructose ... - NCBI - NIH."
https://www.ncbi.nlm.nih.gov/pmc/articles/PMC6032988/.
[62] "Impact of Whole, Fresh Fruit Consumption on ... - Frontiers."
https://www.frontiersin.org/articles/10.3389/fnut.2019.00066/full.

subsidize corn while only $678 million went to apples or vegetables. Corn is used for high fructose corn syrup.

Fructose at the liver does not cause an insulin response to move it into the cell to be used as energy. Fructose metabolism bypasses steps that glucose has to go through. Glucose is directly metabolized widely through the body but fructose is metabolized almost entirely in the liver. Glucose ingestion causes insulin release to lower the glucose in the bloodstream but fructose doesn't cause an insulin release, doesn't affect blood glucose levels and has a low glycemic index. Once in the liver though fructose is metabolized to fructose-1-phosphate primarily by fructokinase or ketohexokinase (KHK). Fructokinase has no negative feedback system, and ATP is used for the phosphorylation process. This process causes the generation of uric acid which is damaging to cells. Fructose-1-phosphate is then metabolized to glyceraldehyde-3-phosphate which enters the mitochondria and then metabolized to Acetyl CoA which then goes into the famous Kreb's Cycle becoming a substrate for lipogenesis. All of this happens in the liver while glucose is being used around the body. Glucose causes insulin release which also causes lipogenesis (fat creation).

Fructose in the liver is not only converted to fat, but causes damage to the mitochondria.[63] Mitochondrial dysfunction has been implicated in a variety of diseases from bipolar disorder, depression, metabolic syndrome, autism and the list goes on because the mitochondria are the power plants of the cell. Just as microbiome research exploded, mitochondrial dysfunction research is exploding, bringing more clarity to disease mechanisms. Fructose is implicated in microbiome dysfunction by "savaging" the intestinal barrier releasing endotoxins, altering gut metabolites and consequently contributing to the progression of non-alcoholic liver disease (NAFLD). Inflammation results from lipogenesis also contributing to NAFLD.[64] Fructose is sweet whereas glucose isn't therefore the sweet taste of fructose drives the consumption and

[63] "Fructose-Rich Diet Affects Mitochondrial DNA Damage and ... - NCBI." https://www.ncbi.nlm.nih.gov/pmc/articles/PMC5409662/.
[64] "Fructose: A Dietary Sugar in Crosstalk with Microbiota ... - NCBI." https://www.ncbi.nlm.nih.gov/pmc/articles/PMC5609573/.

addiction.[65] Fructose commonly appears with glucose in nature while the actions are different, they affect each other.[66] Processing becomes the key determinant of the effects.[67] Fruit contains fructose but the body is able to metabolize it, store or use as energy, but if consumed as high fructose corn syrup which is 55% fructose and 45% glucose or table sugar (50-50 mixture of glucose and fructose) the body deteriorates. The best measure of the deleterious effect is waist to height ratio as fructose preferentially leads to visceral adiposity (belly fat).[68]

[65] "The Small Intestine Converts Dietary Fructose into ... - Cell Press." 6 Feb. 2018, https://www.cell.com/cell-metabolism/abstract/S1550-4131(17)30729-5.

[66] "Fructose metabolism in humans – what isotopic tracer studies ... - NCBI." https://www.ncbi.nlm.nih.gov/pmc/articles/PMC3533803/.

[67] "Controlled study links processed food to increased calorie ...." 16 May. 2019, https://www.eurekalert.org/pub_releases/2019-05/cp-csl050919.php.

[68] "Greater Fructose Consumption Is Associated with ... - NCBI - NIH." https://www.ncbi.nlm.nih.gov/pmc/articles/PMC3260058/.

Reducing Medications

High Blood Pressure

Lisinopril or losartan, hydrochlorothiazide or furosemide, amlodipine and metoprolol are the main medications used to treat high blood pressure. All of them have many side effects. Most people will start with one high blood pressure pill at around 45 years old then another at 55 then by 65 years old will be taking three high blood pressure pills a day to keep it under control. The belly fat around the liver produces substances that raise your pressure so the more belly fat usually the higher the pressure.

There are three businesses that populate our cities. Gas stations that sell junk, fast food junk food stores and dialysis centers. They all go together. Kidney failure is usually caused by people not taking their high blood pressure medicine properly, especially if they have diabetes. It's too much pressure on the kidneys so they become damaged then fail. It's better to Quit, Switch and Sweat...

The guidelines are controversial and appear to not properly take into account low risk patients based upon a study published in December 2018 by Shepherd and others in JAMA.[69] Millions of people are taking blood pressure medications in this category. Those with mild hypertension (defined as 3 consecutive blood pressure readings of 140/90-159/99 mm Hg within 12 months) and low CVD risk identified by excluding anyone with a history of CVD, left ventricular hypertrophy, atrial fibrillation, diabetes, chronic kidney disease, or family history of premature heart disease may not need to be on medications for high blood pressure. The side effects may outweigh the risks.[70]

Another organization, the American Academy of Family Physicians, suggests for those over 60 years old should

[69] "Antihypertensive Treatment and Blood Pressure in Diabetic and ...." 22 Apr. 2011, https://www.ncbi.nlm.nih.gov/pmc/articles/PMC3632197/. 29 Dec. 2018.

[70] "Antihypertensive treatment questionable in mild hypertension - Healio." 29 Oct. 2018, https://www.healio.com/cardiology/vascular-medicine/news/online/%7Bb2a094a8-5e8a-4587-bec9-e58874c44e52%7D/antihypertensive-treatment-questionable-in-mild-hypertension. 29 Dec. 2018.

be medicated if more than 150/90 and the target is reduced to 140/90 for those under 60.[71]

The most accepted guidelines recognized by most physicians are from the American Heart Association jointly with the American College of Cardiology. In 2017 they redefined high blood pressure to be 130/80. This was prehypertensive but now is hypertensive. The evidence they used was heavily based upon a research trial called SPRINT. This was the AAFP's statement:

"The AAFP chose not to participate in this guideline development given significant concerns about the guideline methodology, including the management of intellectual conflicts of interest of guideline participants."[72] The new AHA/ACC guidelines should cut patients risk in half based upon their data and interpretation. The last change was in 1997. Their argument is that 120/80 has always been normal and

---

[71] "AAFP Decides to Not Endorse AHA/ACC Hypertension Guideline." 12 Dec. 2017, https://www.aafp.org/news/health-of-the-public/20171212notendorseaha-accgdlne.html. 29 Dec. 2018.

[72] "AAFP Decides to Not Endorse AHA/ACC Hypertension Guideline." 12 Dec. 2017, https://www.aafp.org/news/health-of-the-public/20171212notendorseaha-accgdlne.html.

they really just changed the classification of who are prehypertensive. Those will now be called Stage 1 hypertensive. So to call them prehypertensive when they are double the risk of heart attacks is too risky based upon the new information particularly for those above 60 years old. For those older, both numbers are important but the main number is the top number: systolic. Stage 2 is now for those above 140/90. Now if someone's blood pressure is either above 180 for the systolic reading or 120 for the diastolic reading then they are in a hypertensive crisis meaning they should go immediately to the emergency room.

The AHA/ACC guidelines actually do not suggest prescribing medications immediately for prehypertension or Stage 1 hypertension unless a patient has already had a cardiovascular event such as a heart attack or stroke, or is at high risk of heart attack or stroke based on age, the presence of diabetes, kidney disease or atherosclerotic risk.[73] For those under 60 the recommendations are not that much different

---

[73] "New ACC/AHA High Blood Pressure ...." 13 Nov. 2017, https://www.acc.org/latest-in-cardiology/articles/2017/11/08/11/47/mon-5pm-bp-guideline-aha-2017.

concerning medications. The AHA/ACC guidelines suggest lifestyle changes.

The major reason the various groups are at odds is based upon different sets of patients being studied. The study by Shepherd only applies to patients without any risk factors. The AAFP group looked at people with diabetes in the ACCORD trial where in diabetes, attempting to achieve blood pressure numbers below 120/80 really does not help and may hurt.[74] Not only in patients with diabetes but for patients with kidney disease, there is a concern if the lower number is less than 70 because acute renal failure becomes a serious risk at those low diastolic numbers.[75] The kidneys need a high enough pressure to function. In contrast though for renal protection, the top number above 130 is a concern in those same patients just like a balloon bursting. The kidneys are extremely sensitive to high

---

[74] "Landmark ACCORD Trial Finds Intensive Blood Pressure and ... - NIH." 15 Mar. 2010, https://www.nih.gov/news-events/news-releases/landmark-accord-trial-finds-intensive-blood-pressure-combination-lipid-therapies-do-not-reduce-combined-cardiovascular-events-adults-diabetes.

[75] "Treatment of Hypertension: Which Goal for Which Patient? - NCBI." https://www.ncbi.nlm.nih.gov/pubmed/27722961.

and low blood pressure numbers which is why there are so many dialysis centers sprouting up everywhere. The SPRINT trial looked at patients with existing cardiovascular disease which showed major differences in patients treated below 120/80 as opposed to 140/90.

Please do not worry about which set of numbers your physician uses to prescribe. Your job is to get the blood pressure numbers low enough to where he/she doesn't have to worry about you having a stroke, heart attack or kidney failure. They are truly trying to protect you and help. Everyone may not be able to reduce their numbers that low but many will. Also, if you have already had a heart attack, stroke, or have diabetes and more then everything changes. Once your organs have been damaged, it is very wise for the medical team to be as cautious as possible in their strategy to protect your life. The key is prevention and QSS can be your focus. 3.2% of all emergency room visits are from a hypertensive crisis and ⅓ of those patients didn't know they had hypertension.[76] It can lead to a heart attack, kidney failure, stroke, and more while any of these can cause immediate death. High blood pressure is serious. Follow the physician's instructions to the letter even if you are a physician. A doctor that treats himself has a fool for a patient. Teamwork is the key and everyone has to do their part. Almost half of the United States has high blood pressure. It can almost always be prevented with QSS.

The last S (Sweat) is critical reflected by a December 2018 study which found that *assuming equally reliable estimates, the SBP-lowering effect of exercise among hypertensive populations appears similar to that of commonly used antihypertensive medications.*[77] Now this doesn't mean we should exercise and stop taking medications. It means exercise and take your

---

[76] "Hypertension, hypertensive emergencies, hypertensive urgency ...."
https://www.renalandurologynews.com/nephrology-hypertension/hypertension-hypertension-crisis-hypertension-hypertensive-emergencies-hypertensive-urgency-malignant-hypertension/article/616204/.
[77] "How does exercise treatment compare with antihypertensive ...." 5 Dec. 2018,
https://bjsm.bmj.com/content/early/2018/12/05/bjsports-2018-099921.

medicines, then you should see your blood pressure decreasing. Remember, any physician will decrease doses or remove medicines when your blood pressure goes too low particularly the top number (systolic). The guidelines suggest moderate intensity exercise for 150 minutes per week (30 minutes, five times a week), or vigorous exercise for 75 minutes per week.[78] Moderate intensity is like walking or slow bicycling and vigorous intensity is like running, fast bicycling or jump rope.[79] Both will make you sweat. We use sweat as an easy way to get people moving. Sweat is not a physiologically good determinant of exercise intensity but it is probably the most powerful illustrator of activity.[80] Exercise does wonders for the body and mind including helping the body to communicate with itself to enhance cell

---

[78] "Physical Activity Guidelines for Americans | HHS.gov." https://www.hhs.gov/fitness/be-active/physical-activity-guidelines-for-americans/index.html.

[79] "Moderate to Vigorous - What is your level of intensity?." http://www.heart.org/HEARTORG/HealthyLiving/PhysicalActivity/FitnessBasics/Moderate-to-Vigorous-What-is-your-level-of-intensity_UCM_463775_Article.jsp?appName=MobileApp.

[80] "Trapped sweat in basketball uniforms and the effect on sweat ... - NCBI." 27 Sep. 2017, https://www.ncbi.nlm.nih.gov/pubmed/28963129.

efficiencies.[81] Exercise also affects proteins or the proteome which describes a complicated network that keeps the entire body in balance.[82] Exercise is better than many drugs for many conditions but doesn't really work for weight loss.[83] Aerobic exercise helps for belly fat, but not too much for weight.[84] If you are looking to lose weight, you must QSS or else if you sweat without the Q and the first S - you'll get frustrated from a lack of results. So many people work out and seemingly eat less but still eat sweets, soft drinks and white bread sandwiches. They spend hard earned money in the gym but nothing changes. They will then end up on medication or having it increased even with a lot of sweating and hard work. That is frustrating. Reduce belly fat first, then reduce medications.

---

[81] "Extracellular Vesicles: A Novel Target for Exercise ... - NCBI - NIH." 19 June. 2018, https://www.ncbi.nlm.nih.gov/pmc/articles/PMC6029462/.
[82] "exercise - American Journal of Physiology." https://www.physiology.org/doi/10.1152/japplphysiol.00458.2018.
[83] "Aerobic exercise but not resistance exercise reduces ... - NCBI - NIH." https://www.ncbi.nlm.nih.gov/pmc/articles/PMC3840217/.
[84] "The Effects of Exercise and Physical Activity on Weight Loss ... - NCBI." 9 July. 2018, https://www.ncbi.nlm.nih.gov/pubmed/30003901.

In summary, you must know your blood pressure numbers so purchase a blood pressure cuff. They should cost about $40 but will truly help you and your physician. The numbers can really change depending upon the amount of stress you are under, such as when you walk into a doctor's office. Taking the pressure at home regularly will give you and the medical team a better picture of your blood pressure over time.

The key points when taking your pressure at home:

- Wait 5 minutes to relax before taking your pressure
- Wait 30 minutes after exercising, smoking, drinking coffee, Red Bull or other caffeinated drinks
- Sit in a chair that supports your back as opposed to a sofa
- Keep feet flat on floor
- Be still, quiet and talk after taking pressure. Your arm should be on a flat surface like a table at heart level
- Place cuff above bottom bend of the elbow on your skin (not over clothes)

- Take 2 or 3 readings each time and record them along with time and date.
- Record online or by paper, but bring it to your doctor at each visit.

Talking to your doctor while they take your pressure can make the top number rise by 9 mmHg. It returns in about 5 minutes to normal though.[85] White coat hypertension is real. The actual best solution is 24 hour blood pressure monitoring. Too high and too low can both be a problem so this gives the absolute best picture, better than even doctor's office readings, and is cost effective in the long run. One study described that it was excellent particularly for the elderly and obese, those with secondary or resistant hypertension, and those diagnosed with diabetes, kidney disease, metabolic syndrome, and sleep disorders.[86] A good wrist wearable device runs about $50 but is well worth

---

[85] "Talking with a doctor during a visit elicits increases in systolic ... - NCBI." https://www.ncbi.nlm.nih.gov/pubmed/28723834.
[86] "[2013 Ambulatory blood pressure monitoring recommendations ... - NCBI." https://www.ncbi.nlm.nih.gov/pubmed/23849214.

it if someone is at risk. Usually wrist devices are not as accurate, but for 24 hour monitoring, they work as well as arm devices.[87]

---

[87] "Comparison of wrist-type and arm-type 24-h blood pressure ... - NCBI." https://www.ncbi.nlm.nih.gov/pubmed/23263536.

	Normal	Pre hypertensive	Stage 1	Stage 2	Crisis Top #	Crisis Bottom #
AHA/ ACC	<120/80	120/80-129/80	Top 130-139 Bottom 80-89	>140/90	> 180	>120
AAFP/ JNC 8	<120/80	120/80-139-89	Under 60: Top 140-159 Bottom 90-99 Over 60 Top: 150-159	Top >160 Bottom >100	>180	>120

Remember there are many reasons why a physician may choose your target so follow. As Dr. Milton Packer stated, "Guidelines represent the opinions of its authors. Nothing more and nothing less. Their text is worth reading, but the document should not be the focus of worship. Guidelines are not biblical scripture." [88] In fact the leading voice today who serves as a prophetic messenger for researchers declares that professional societies should remove themselves from

[88] "When Did Guidelines Become Holy Writ? | Medpage Today." 17 Oct. 2018, https://www.medpagetoday.com/blogs/revolutionandrevelation/757 52.

writing guidelines because of inherent conflicts of interest.[89] Dr. John Ioannidis is one of the most highly cited researchers in the world, but is fighting against huge financial interests and established dogma. For the patient, the risks are huge. For an adult 45 years of age without hypertension, the 40-year risk for developing hypertension is 93% for African Americans, 92% for Hispanics, 86% for whites, and 84% for Chinese adults. [90] High blood pressure is the most dominant factor in heart disease and strokes, which kill more people far more than any other disease.

Salt is a controversial issue as it has been called public enemy number one. Just like with blood pressure wars, there are salt wars. In January of 2018 the Atlantic and the New York Times published articles about scientists desiring to study prisoners to find out the optimum salt

---

[89] "Professional Societies Should Abstain From ... - AHA Journals." 2 Oct. 2018, https://www.ahajournals.org/doi/pdf/10.1161/CIRCOUTCOMES.11 8.004889.
[90] "2017 Guideline for High Blood Pressure in Adults - American College ...." 7 May. 2018, https://www.acc.org/latest-in-cardiology/ten-points-to-remember/20 17/11/09/11/41/2017-guideline-for-high-blood-pressure-in-adults.

intake. They were serious and seriously cruel.[91] How could they? The issue is complex though because just like in the blood pressure numbers you may get a J or U shaped curve in the graph meaning that some are helped and some or hurt by lower targets.[92] [93] The arguments are strong on both sides with the same cardiologists (ACC) from the blood pressure wars staking their case that lower sodium is best for everyone.[94] A 2018 Lancet article showed only salt intake above 12.5 grams a day (5 grams a day of sodium) was associated with stroke and cardiovascular disease.[95] This is much much more than the

---

[91] "The Ideal Subjects for a Salt Study? Maybe Prisoners - The New York ...." 4 Jun. 2018, https://www.nytimes.com/2018/06/04/health/prisoners-salt-study.html.

[92] "Association between sodium intake and CV events characterized by U ...." 20 Aug. 2018, https://ipccs.org/2018/08/20/association-between-sodium-intake-and-cv-events-characterized-by-u-shaped-curve/.

[93] "How Robust Is the Evidence for Recommending Very Low Salt ... - NCBI." 11 Oct. 2016, https://www.ncbi.nlm.nih.gov/pubmed/27712773.

[94] "Sodium Intake and All-Cause Mortality over 20 Years in ... - NCBI - NIH." 11 Oct. 2017, https://www.ncbi.nlm.nih.gov/pmc/articles/PMC5098805/

[95] "Urinary sodium excretion, blood pressure, cardiovascular ... - The Lancet." 11 Aug. 2018,

recommended 1500 to 2000 mg of sodium but it is at the higher end of what most people eat - between 3 to 5 grams a day. The optimum levels would be 2800 to 6000 mg per day.[96] The American Heart Association recommends 2300 mg a day and 1500 mg a day for those with hypertension even suggesting that 1000 mg a day would be better.[97] The issue is that the scientists that are recommending high intakes admit that lower intakes lowers blood pressure, but their argument is that lower salt intake causes other detrimental things to happen in the body leading to heart attacks, strokes and death.

My recommendation is always real food seasoned to taste. Processed foods are the problem.[98] Processed restaurant foods account for 70% of salt intake, 14% comes from naturally occurring sodium and the

https://www.thelancet.com/journals/lancet/article/PIIS0140-6736(18)31376-X/fulltext.

[96] "Making Sense of the Science of Sodium - NCBI - NIH." 26 Mar. 2015, https://www.ncbi.nlm.nih.gov/pmc/articles/PMC4420256/.

[97] "How much sodium should I eat per day ...." https://sodiumbreakup.heart.org/how_much_sodium_should_i_eat.

[98] "The Bulk of US Salt Intake Comes From Processed Foods - CardioSmart." 15 Jun. 2017, https://www.cardiosmart.org/News-and-Events/2017/06/The-Bulk-of-US-Salt-Intake-Comes-From-Processed-Foods.

remainder only comes from the shaker used during cooking or at the table. We just have to eat real food. QSS would do it. It's rare to find high salt foods without sugar or refined carbs. Eating real, unprocessed food makes it easier to reach any salt target. Reducing medications all goes back to eating nourishing food.

Deprescribing is the goal but as you can see compliance is a must. The villain is not your doctor but profit driven drug companies and big food companies. Drug companies fund 75% of drug trials and the situation smells very bad. Their money is everywhere. The health professionals that see patients are only cogs in a big financial wheel dependent upon the information presented. What should people do? Trust your physician or find another one. More important is to find a very knowledgeable pharmacist that specializes in deprescribing to navigate the process.[99] It is a very tight rope with disaster all over but it can be done. Many people just don't take the medications and then end up

---

[99] "Impact of pharmacist's intervention on disease related ... - NCBI." https://www.ncbi.nlm.nih.gov/pubmed/30587468.

paying the funeral director. I see it everyday where people will skip doses and not take entire regimens. Over 60% don't take medicine properly[100] and one third don't even get their prescriptions filled.[101] People are deprescribing on their own without communicating with anyone and many times trying to hide it. They'll start taking their pills before going to a check-up. Teamwork makes the dreamwork. The pharmacist should drive this ship but in the retail chains they are run like horses trying to meet the speed and profit numbers.[102] The system is not set up to get people off of medication. They would lose money. It is not even set up to know what the patient should be on. No one usually knows unless the patient only sees one

---

[100] "Report shows over 60 percent of Americans don't follow doctors ...." 25 Apr. 2012, https://scopeblog.stanford.edu/2012/04/25/report-shows-over-60-percent-of-americans-dont-follow-doctors-orders-in-taking-prescription-meds/.

[101] "Primary Nonadherence With Prescribed Medication in Primary Care ...." 1 Apr. 2014, http://annals.org/aim/fullarticle/1852865/incidence-determinants-primary-nonadherence-prescribed-medication-primary-care-cohort-study.

[102] "How Chaos at Chain Pharmacies Is Putting Patients at Risk ...." https://www.nytimes.com/2020/01/31/health/pharmacists-medication-errors.html.

physician and even then they don't know about the supplements and herbs that the patient takes which are all drugs, yes drugs. The pharmacy software has an automatic system that once a prescription comes to the pharmacy by electronic means or by paper - it just fills every refill then calls the doctor automatically when out of refills so the pharmacy keeps getting paid. There is no system to take you off of the medicine. If you are seeing multiple doctors, not one knows what the other doctors are prescribing even when certain clinics and hospitals have a so called central database because there is no acceptable quality control system and errors are everywhere. Regardless of the systems no one is asking the question. Doctors ask the patient what they are on or tell them to bring their prescription bottles to the doctor's office. Physicians or nurses will call the pharmacy to get their incomplete list since many patients use multiple pharmacies. The culture of compartmentalized medicine keeps doctors from checking on other doctor's decisions anyway. It is extremely rare that one doctor will question another doctor's prescribing. Everyone stays in their lane. The patient is almost always told to go back for an office visit. They don't want to take the drug anyway. The pharmacist has no idea since they just fill what comes in. The so called MTM or Medication Therapy Management system that certain patients are selected for, where the pharmacist consults with the patient and educates them along with checking for drug interactions has nothing to do with contacting each physician to verify what the patient should be on. The data comes from the insurance company database and the pharmacist asks the patient who usually can't even pronounce the medications let alone know why they're prescribed. No one knows. The patient is just taking pills. Insurance companies know what is billed but it doesn't catch what's not filled which is the real problem. They key in on certain drugs but no one is looking at the complete therapy let alone diet, exercise, sleep, sex, or social connections. Rarely can a pharmacist even speak with a physician directly about therapy. No one has time or is paid to have the conversation. The doctor tells the patient about a drug whose information came from a drug representative, conference or research trial all sponsored by a drug company whose goal is profit. The pharmacist fills the prescription but has no idea of the conversation with the physician. The patient probably hadn't studied medicinal chemistry or even biochemistry and is in no position to evaluate or understand what the physician is doing or the drug company's involvement and they don't want to take it anyway. Many who take them think they are candy and not realizing they are like a cannon to the body. Most kidney failures and congestive heart failures are caused by not taking the medication properly. Heart disease and stroke kill almost a million people a year, many more than cancer or anything else. We began using a blister system but it isn't the packaging system, it is taking the time to talk with everyone about what this patient should be on and controlling the process. We send the blisters out and within a few weeks patients give up total control and just take what we provide in the packs. They love it because regardless of the level of education, the bottle system doesn't work for anyone taking more than 4 medications a day. We obtain prescriptions for "over the counter" drugs taken regularly and add them to the blister packs, taking full responsibility for drug interactions, appropriateness of use, side effect issues, proper timing of doses, drug food interactions and more. This is real pharmacy. The problem is getting the information from the physicians. They are too busy and the nurses have limited information as to the thought process the physician used in prescribing the medication. We add in nutrition, sleep, and total lifestyle to give a complete wellness service. We also provide QSS meals a la carte or through weekly meal plans. We are Best Life Pharmacy and Restaurant but truly caring for people demands this level of service. What good is medicine without the food?

My aunt had a 2nd stroke but this one paralyzed both legs and one arm. That non-paralyzed arm was incapacitated by parkinson's disease. My mom wanted to care for her at home as she did for the 1st stroke, so I offered. She was given 6 months to live and placed on hospice. I traveled 25 minutes there twice a day to feed her, bathe her and ensure she had bowel movements. The stroke and being bedridden restricted her bowel function. She could only accept liquids and drinking was a very slow process. Clocked in many hours a day in the beginning until we finally found 2 home health aides that were consistent and caring enough to make an impact. If she didn't get proper care bed sores would happen quickly so we always knew when we could back off. Bowel function had to be consistent too. Quality aides took about 4 years to find but instead of her living 6 months she lived 13 years! Only Katrina really challenged her when we had to move her to a nursing home and even then she lived about a year and a half after. God is amazing. We'll discuss Him more later but high blood pressure damages the blood vessels creating the conditions for blockages in the heart, kidney and brain particularly. When the pressure is high in the vessels, they become narrow causing more pressure. The high pressure is caused by oxidative stress.[103] [104] That's why antioxidants are talked about so much because they clean it up (reduce oxidation) but you

---

[103] "Oxidative Stress and Hypertensive Diseases. - NCBI - NIH." 27 Oct. 2016, https://www.ncbi.nlm.nih.gov/pubmed/27884227.
[104] "Vascular Endothelial Function and Hypertension: Insights ... - NCBI - NIH."
https://www.ncbi.nlm.nih.gov/pmc/articles/PMC2982873/.

can't get their benefit from a pill. They have to come from food.[105] When belly fat is present, the fat around the organs produce substances (adipocytokines) that cause inflammation in the body and also in those arterial blood vessels. Fat, cholesterol along with other substances normally present in the oxygen rich blood from food and produced by the body form plaque that builds up in the presence of inflamed blood vessels. The LDL particle size is a major issue because different foods lead to different particle sizes. The fat and cholesterol can't move around the body because they repel water so they are attached to a protein and called a lipoprotein. Low density lipoprotein is the main one that carries cholesterol through the body. The high density lipoprotein takes away cholesterol and brings it back to the liver. Remember the first Q is quitting sodas and sweets. Sugars and refined carbohydrates lead to small particle size LDL cholesterol which is able to

---

[105] "Antioxidants: In Depth | NCCIH."
https://nccih.nih.gov/health/antioxidants/introduction.htm.

penetrate the vessel lining to form plaques more than large particle LDL.[106]

The gut contains tens of trillions of microorganisms which are many more than the cells in our bodies. The majority are found in the part of the large intestine called the cecum but those found in the small intestine are extremely important also.[107] The organisms within their environment together is called a microbiome. The organisms are called a microbiota. In fact there is a microbiome within the brain, vagina, mouth and more... When they are out of balance in the gut they cause inflammation also leading to and accelerating atherosclerosis (plaque build-up).[108] They are also directly affected by diet. Artificial sweeteners are toxic to the gut microbiome.[109] They love fiber from grains,

---

[106] "Influence of dietary carbohydrate and fat on LDL and HDL ... - NCBI." https://www.ncbi.nlm.nih.gov/pubmed/16256003.

[107] "The human small intestinal microbiota is driven by rapid ... - NCBI - NIH." 19 Jan. 2012, https://www.ncbi.nlm.nih.gov/pmc/articles/PMC3379644/.

[108] "A Pro-Inflammatory Gut Microbiota Increases Systemic ... - NCBI." https://www.ncbi.nlm.nih.gov/pubmed/30582442.

[109] "Molecules | Free Full-Text | Effects of the Artificial Sweetener ... - MDPI." 9 Feb. 2018, https://www.mdpi.com/1420-3049/23/2/367.

fruits and vegetables[110], but hate sodas, sweets and refined carbohydrates (white carbs). The big question is the role of LDL in the creation of the blockages. It makes a big difference because when we discuss taking statin drugs, LDL is the focus. It was necessary to discuss LDL along with blood pressure drugs because everything is related. It starts with sodas, sweets, white bread, white rice and white pasta. And yes of course large amounts of fat matters. We'll discuss later in the statin wars.

---

[110] "Carbohydrate quality and human health: a series of ... - The Lancet."
https://www.thelancet.com/journals/lancet/article/PIIS0140-6736(18)31809-9/fulltext.

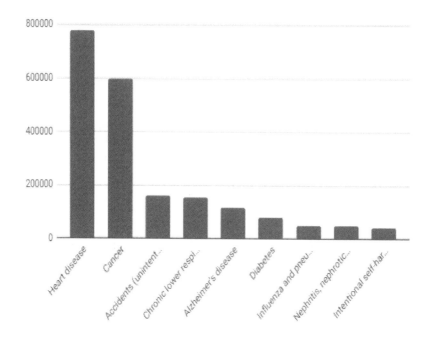

High cholesterol

Usually when you're around 60 years old while on the second blood pressure pill doctors may prescribe a statin drug and its usually atorvastatin. The big news is that we are in the middle of the statin wars concerning those who haven't had a heart attack or stroke. The big camps are from the British Medical Journal and the Lancet with lawsuits and name calling all around.[111] Also the same group from the hypertension numbers: the ACC/AHA is involved again along with the US Preventive Services Task Force (USPSTF) challenging their numbers.[112] The statin wars involve the patient much more than any of the other wars because physicians are supposed to involve patients in the discussion since it involves how much risk they may want to take. The argument is mainly about giving these

---

[111] "Lessons from the controversy over statins - The Lancet." https://www.thelancet.com/journals/lancet/article/PIIS0140-6736(17)30721-3/fulltext.

[112] "Comparison of Recommended Eligibility for ... - The JAMA Network." 18 Apr. 2017, https://jamanetwork.com/journals/jama/fullarticle/2618621.

pills to people who are healthy to prevent an anticipated heart attack. Of course if over 40 and your LDL is over 190, or have diabetes or any kind of cardiovascular disease then you will be prescribed a statin. The first question though concerns the use of a 10 year risk calculator that plugs in:

Gender_____
Age_____
Race_____
Total Cholesterol_____
LDL Cholesterol_____
HDL Cholesterol_____
Treatment With Statin - Yes or No
Systolic (top number) Blood Pressure_____
Treatment For Hypertension - Yes or No
History Of Diabetes - Yes or No
Current Smoker - Yes or No
Aspirin Therapy - Yes or No

The recommendations from ACC/AHA suggest having a statin conversation if your LDL is over 70 but with no other risk factor than a 10 year risk score of 7.5% or more. Your cardiovascular disease 10 year risk will be over 7.5% when 61 years old if a white male and 62 if a black male if other indices were: blood pressure 120/80, HDL: 50, LDL: 70, TC: 185, never smoked, no history of diabetes and not on a statin or hypertension medication or aspirin. Looking at the higher age for black men, it is not that black men have a lower risk of heart disease, but actually their risk is higher, therefore if a black man hasn't had any issues by that age then their risk would be lower. Regardless, they will be placed on a statin. Women have estrogen protection and more so they live longer and wouldn't get to over a 7.5% risk for many more years than men - 69 for white women and 67 for black women. Again assuming all other indices are the same as above. The calculator only works for those under 79 years old but discontinuation of statin use in 75 year olds was associated with a 33% increase in hospital admission for cardiovascular events in a French study.[113] Deprescribing is complex.

The USPSTF recommends that statins be prescribed only if other risk factors are present such as diabetes, high blood pressure or smoking regardless of age,

---

[113] "Cardiovascular effect of discontinuing statins for ... - NCBI." https://www.ncbi.nlm.nih.gov/pubmed/31362307.

which would delay or prevent millions from people taking statins. It would take 250 people taking statins for 1 to 6 years for one death to be prevented.[114] Data also shows that reducing LDL levels below 130 mg/dl isn't necessary in high cardiovascular risk patients anyway.[115] They have side effects which are mainly muscle weakness but some may develop memory problems,[116] [117] liver problems, kidney problems, and/or diabetes.[118] The memory issue is controversial and shouldn't affect the prescribing of the drug. Even for diabetes, statin use may be warranted[119] since again, heart attacks and strokes are the number one cause of

[114] "Statins for Prevention of Cardiovascular Disease ... - The JAMA Network." 15 Nov. 2016, https://jamanetwork.com/journals/jama/fullarticle/2584057.
[115] "Narrative review: lack of evidence for recommended low ... - NCBI - NIH." 3 Oct. 2006, https://www.ncbi.nlm.nih.gov/pubmed/17015870.
[116] "Statins: The Burglar of Memory? - NCBI." 1 Dec. 2018, https://www.ncbi.nlm.nih.gov/pubmed/30545434.
[117] "Is statin-associated cognitive impairment clinically relevant? A ... - NCBI." 3 Apr. 2012, https://www.ncbi.nlm.nih.gov/pubmed/22474137.
[118] "diabetes AND statins - PubMed Result - NCBI." https://www.ncbi.nlm.nih.gov/sites/entrez/?term=diabetes+AND+statins.
[119] "Is statin-associated cognitive impairment clinically relevant? A ... - NCBI." 3 Apr. 2012, https://www.ncbi.nlm.nih.gov/pubmed/22474137.

death worldwide so much more than anything else. It's all about risks and low risk patients can be removed or not put on in the first place.[120]

There are many tests that your physician will review before having the statin conversation. They'll be looking at:

1) Persistently elevated LDL over 160 mg/dl. Even though your LDL is not yet 190, but even if over 160, it increases your risk and should be a part of the conversation.

3) Chronic kidney disease is usually caused by diabetes and/or high blood pressure, but if the patient is over 75 years old, it may not factor in as much.

4) Early menopause is a concern since women would lose estrogen protection earlier.

---

[120] "Statin Therapy: Diabetes Mellitus Risk and Cardiovascular ... - NCBI." https://www.ncbi.nlm.nih.gov/pubmed/30084572.

5) Family history of premature ASCVD. Genetics does play a part but families also have similar recipes, exercise habits, incomes, stress levels and access to healthcare.

6) Chronic inflammatory disorders (HIV, rheumatoid arthritis, psoriasis). Cardiovascular disease is thought to be mainly an inflammatory disease[121] so obviously a person with immune system challenges would be more at risk.

7) South Asian descent meaning people from India, Pakistan, Sri Lanka, Nepal and Bangladesh. Whether it is genetic or lifestyle is in question, but they represent a ¼ of the developing world and have cardiovascular disease at a much higher rate.

8) Low ankle-brachial index is an interesting indicator. It measures the difference in pressure between the ankle and the arm. If there is lower blood pressure in

---

[121] "Inflammation, not Cholesterol, Is a Cause of Chronic ... - NCBI - NIH." https://www.ncbi.nlm.nih.gov/pmc/articles/PMC5986484/.

the ankle it represents blockage or narrowing of arteries in your legs. The blockage would disrupt the blood flow to that area therefore lowering the pressure.

9) Persistently elevated TG (≥175). Your body changes soft drinks and sweets (simple carbs) to triglycerides which are a form of fat in the blood. Fat from oily fish reduces triglycerides.

10) Lp(a) is an indicator interestingly difficult to change but more studies are needed.[122]

11) ApoB and particularly the ratio between ApoA1 and ApoB gives a better measure of cardiovascular disease risk than LDL but LDL is used more. ApoB measures LDL particles and ApoA1 measures HDL particles and it is the number of LDL particles compared to HDL particles that are problematic. LDL can be high but if the particle size is large then the risk isn't higher than if the particle size was low. Small LDL particles enter the

---

[122] "Lipoprotein(a): Biology and Clinical Importance - NCBI - NIH." https://www.ncbi.nlm.nih.gov/pmc/articles/PMC1853362/.

arterial wall leading to the plaque buildup[123] which becomes calcified (hard) over time. The clinical relevance of triglycerides or LDL cholesterol are both dependent upon ApoB particles.[124]

12) HsCRP measures the level of inflammation. Inflammation is the key, but other types of inflammation may affect the number.

The statin conversation is really about eating and exercise because truly if they are out of balance then the numbers will move higher and many times fast. If your 10 year heart attack risk score is over 7.5% but under 19.9% with LDL over 70 and still unsure about starting statins, your physician may order a coronary artery calcium score. Calcium builds up in the plaque and can be measured with a non-invasive CT scan. If the score is

---

[123] "Small Dense Low-Density Lipoprotein as Biomarker for ... - NCBI - NIH." 12 Apr. 2017, https://www.ncbi.nlm.nih.gov/pmc/articles/PMC5441126/.
[124] "Association of Triglyceride-Lowering LPL Variants ... - JAMA Network.", https://jamanetwork.com/journals/jama/fullarticle/2722770.

low then you may delay beginning statins for 5 years or more.

The discussion is a major conversation with a lot at stake. There are many items to review to get a view of the risks based upon the evidence. Statins only lower risks and are preventative but heart attacks are deadly. Of course there are those who believe that LDL is irrelevant but I'm not convinced. Healthy eating and exercise lowers it anyway. Switching to brown from white is powerful because whole grains lower cholesterol along with fruits, vegetables and beans. Belly fat increases cholesterol. Reduce belly fat and therefore reduce cholesterol. Sugars and refined foods add belly fat more than others and also cause the production of the worst type of LDL cholesterol which has a small particle size that again, allows them to slip into the blood vessel cell wall leading to inflammation and clots. Regardless of changes in suspected mechanisms of disease, real food has been solid for thousands of years.

The cholesterol conversation is the most difficult because it is a risk reduction drug but thankfully the guidelines mandate that the patient participates in the decision to take the risks. There are no guidelines on deprescribing. Inherently if a patient is at low risk and have already been prescribed statins but change their mind or have another conversation, then the physician would have to make their case to continue. God forbid the patient was prescribed without any conversation about risks and chose to take the medication. 45% actually are prescribed and do not take them and many more take them less than prescribed which is not good. Patients should be honest with their physician and discuss their plans. Physicians usually just increase the dose thinking that the lower dose did not work when in fact it would have worked if the drug was taken as prescribed. The statin issue, more than any other issue requires a team approach because of its complexity. I can imagine a fearful, elderly patient without any knowledge of science trying to understand and engage. They need a team backing them that knows them and can help them assess the risks.

High Blood Sugar

Type 2 Diabetes is the easiest major disease in which to reduce medications but the most damaging if allowed to progress. TNF alpha is a substance produced by belly fat that appears to be the main culprit in causing insulin resistance, where insulin resistance is the dominant cause of type 2 diabetes.[125] The pancreas tries to keep up by producing more insulin but the cells in the body are resistant to the insulin. Eventually the pancreas gets worn out... Too much belly fat will do it. A person can be slim but have a belly and be a diabetic. Shape counts more than weight and not just for being attractive but for health. It's actually the fat around the organs that spews out various inflammatory substances like a fountain but this fat pushes out leading to a big belly. The name is visceral fat as opposed to subcutaneous fat (fat under the skin) which you can pinch.

---

[125] "The role of TNF-alpha in insulin resistance. - NCBI." https://www.ncbi.nlm.nih.gov/pubmed/15146098.

Type 2 diabetes is the focus in deprescribing because type 1 diabetes is defined by the beta cells of the pancreas being attacked by the body's own immune system eventually leading to failure of those beta cells. We'll talk about the theological concepts later but heart failure, kidney failure and pancreatic beta cell failure and others will always require medication. The patient is alive but when organ systems fail, medications prevent death. The controversy in type 2 diabetics is at what extent of pancreatic beta cell dysfunction can the beta cell recover when the visceral fat is decreased? The next question is how much visceral fat needs to be removed to observe changes in beta cell function or amount? Caloric restriction normalizes beta cell function as fat is decreased in the liver and pancreas but caloric restriction alone without addressing caloric quality fails long term.[126]

Until 1977 type 1 diabetes was called juvenile onset diabetes because it affected children and type 2 diabetes affected adults. The names were changed because

---

[126] "Reversal of type 2 diabetes: normalisation of beta cell ... - NCBI - NIH." 9 Jun. 2011, https://www.ncbi.nlm.nih.gov/pmc/articles/PMC3168743/.

adults can develop type 1 and children can develop type 2. 95% of diabetics are type 2 but 5-15% of those are misdiagnosed and actually have type 1.[127] We are now beginning to understand that differences between them are less black and white and more gray.[128] Immune system activity is common in both. What's important is that the high blood sugar (that occurs because the beta cells of the pancreas cannot produce enough insulin) causes severe damage to blood vessels and major organs of the body. High blood sugar attacks the body 5 main ways:

1. Glucose (sugar) is turned into sorbitol. It's called the polyol pathway which when activated by an overload of glucose causes cell damage. Sorbitol cannot get into cells causing an imbalance in the cells of other substances. Everything must be in balance for the cells to work. The end result is

---

[127] "Differentiation of Diabetes by Pathophysiology, Natural ... - NCBI - NIH."
https://www.ncbi.nlm.nih.gov/pmc/articles/PMC5384660/.
[128] "Beta cells in type 1 diabetes - Springer Link."
https://link.springer.com/article/10.1007/s00125-019-4822-4.

oxidative stress and AGE's which damage the cell.[129]

2. Glucose causes the production of AGE's (advanced glycation end products). This is the glycation pathway. AGE's alter the structure and function of body proteins and cell membranes causing inflammation and oxidative stress. Oxidation is normal but when overloaded it causes major damage to the cells of the body. Inflammation can be a friend or a foe. When you get a cut, inflammation is helpful, but as a foe it can lead to cell damage within blood vessels, fat tissue and every system of the body.[130] Cardiovascular disease is thought to be an inflammatory disease. AGEs are naturally present in uncooked animal foods, but cooking them causes the formation of new AGEs such as in grilling, broiling, roasting, searing, and frying.

[129] "Polyol Pathway - an overview | ScienceDirect Topics." https://www.sciencedirect.com/topics/medicine-and-dentistry/polyol-pathway.
[130] "Low-grade inflammation, diet composition and health ... - NCBI - NIH." https://www.ncbi.nlm.nih.gov/pmc/articles/PMC4579563/.

Free sugars and meat products produce the most AGE's with plant based whole foods producing the least.[131] Balance is the key.

3. Protein kinase c pathway (PKC) activation is a major way high glucose causes damage. PKC enzymes are involved in increasing oxidation, controlling other proteins, causing vascular changes, cell death, cell growth and so much more. PKC inhibitors are being researched to positively affect diabetic eye disease, nerve disease and kidney disease.[132] PKC enzymes may affect cells directly or through oxidation which is caused by the imbalance of reactive oxygen species. They are truly reactive causing damage to proteins, DNA, and lipids (fat) in huge chemical chain reactions damaging cell functions.

4. Hexosamine pathway activation damages the pancreatic beta cells themselves which produce

[131] "Advanced Glycation End Products in Foods ...."
https://www.ncbi.nlm.nih.gov/pmc/articles/PMC3704564/.
[132] "Activation of Protein Kinase C Isoforms & Its Impact on ... - NCBI - NIH."
https://www.ncbi.nlm.nih.gov/pmc/articles/PMC2877591/.

the insulin to control the glucose. It creates this vicious cycle of high glucose, high insulin then beta cell failure, low insulin and super high glucose.[133] The roles of oxidative stress and inflammation cannot be minimized since they interact together and individually with all systems creating cellular and system damage.[134] [135]

5. Enediol/alpha-ketoaldehyde pathway activation by high glucose involves chemical reactions oxidizing glucose.[136] The oxidized glucose is converted to an enediol radical anion and through a series of reactions becomes a reactive oxygen species so glucose itself becomes the source of the oxidative stress. All of the pathways involve oxidative stress as the convergence of

---

[133] "Hexosamine pathway but not interstitial changes mediates ... - NCBI." https://www.ncbi.nlm.nih.gov/pubmed/24704640.
[134] "Natural history of β-cell adaptation and failure in type 2 ... - NCBI - NIH." 24 Dec. 2014, https://www.ncbi.nlm.nih.gov/pmc/articles/PMC4404183/.
[135] "Does the Interdependence between Oxidative Stress and ... - Hindawi." 19 Nov. 2015, https://www.hindawi.com/journals/omcl/2016/5698931/.
[136] "Hyperglycemic Stress and Carbon Stress in Diabetic ... - NCBI - NIH." https://www.ncbi.nlm.nih.gov/pmc/articles/PMC4723237/.

chemical reactions. These unpaired electrons are like little bombs that react to important chemicals in the body creating changes and damage. They are quite normal, but become stressful when out of balance with antioxidants. [137]

High blood sugar then creates so much damage to the entire body but particularly blood vessels so that it greatly increases risks for major organ failure. The heart, kidneys and the brain are the big three that are highly susceptible to the effects of too much glucose in the blood. The strangest thing in the world is how type 2 diabetes is treated. The disease is almost totally preventable and even once diabetes develops, it can be practically reversed. Instead of focusing on preventing or reversing, 99% of the effort is placed on using medicine to lower the blood sugar. It's like an oil leak in my car. I keep adding oil but eventually the engine will fail because I will never be able to keep the engine's oil

[137] "Redox imbalance stress in diabetes mellitus: Role of the ... - NCBI - NIH." 19 Apr. 2018, https://www.ncbi.nlm.nih.gov/pmc/articles/PMC5975374/.

at the correct level. Why not just fix the gasket and stop the leak. It costs $80 instead of a $15,000 car. Why not fix the insulin resistance problem instead of adding more insulin. The cost to care for diabetes is about $16,750 yearly and it tops cancer, asthma and all other diseases.[138] [139] That's a new car each year.

The job of the pancreas is to produce insulin to lower the sugar in the blood that varies based upon what we eat. Insulin is produced by the beta cells of the Islets of Langerhans. They were named after Paul Langerhans discovered them in 1869. We now know that they contain 5 different types of cells with the beta cell being the most researched since they secrete insulin. The alpha cells secrete glucagon which balances out insulin's actions but they are the less noticed of the two.

[138] "Economic Costs of Diabetes in the U.S. in 2017 | Diabetes Care."
http://care.diabetesjournals.org/content/early/2018/03/20/dci18-0007.
[139] "The Rising Cost Of Diabetes Care - Optum."
https://www.optum.com/resources/library/rising-cost-diabetes-care.html.

[140] The body always seeks homeostasis or a perfect balance and body systems contain complex mechanisms to make it happen. The alpha and beta cells are a prime example. There will be more to come on the alpha cells but the beta cells are the focus as they secrete insulin which unlocks the cell door to allow glucose to enter the cell and be used to produce energy but insulin does so much more. Insulin suppresses the production of glucose by the liver. It stops fat breakdown and release into the bloodstream. It manages liver metabolism of lipoproteins (such as ApoB, LDL, HDL) which is critical to understanding how diabetics are more prone to cardiovascular disease. [141] Insulin regulates blood lipid removal as well as potently inhibiting the breakdown of proteins.[142] Insulin homeostasis is critical but when the cells become

---

[140] "Pancreatic α-Cell Dysfunction in Type 2 Diabetes: Old ... - NCBI - NIH." 16 Feb. 2015, https://www.ncbi.nlm.nih.gov/pmc/articles/PMC4342530/.
[141] "The Regulation of ApoB Metabolism by Insulin - NCBI - NIH." 27 May. 2013, https://www.ncbi.nlm.nih.gov/pmc/articles/PMC3810413/.
[142] "Metabolic actions of insulin in men and women - NCBI - NIH." 14 Apr. 2010, https://www.ncbi.nlm.nih.gov/pmc/articles/PMC2893237/.

resistant to the insulin, damage ensues. Everything can be solved with nourishing foods which work to decrease belly fat and also does not dump glucose loads in the blood which causes the beta cells to overproduce insulin. The beta cells are highly sensitive to excess glucose so when the overload becomes regularly toxic, those beta cells become dysfunctional and eventually fail. Highly sensitive means quick to fail when overloaded.[143] Sodas and sweets dump loads of sugar along with white bread, white rice, and white pasta. QSS is the key. Nearly half of adults are affected by insulin resistance and either are prediabetic or diabetic. [144] [145] Fat that cannot be used can be stored in subcutaneous tissue but excess carbohydrates can only be converted in the liver to triglycerides. As the fat in the liver builds, it causes liver insulin resistance leading to more insulin to control the glucose produced by the

---

[143] "The islet beta-cell: fuel responsive and vulnerable. - NCBI." 6 Sep. 2008, https://www.ncbi.nlm.nih.gov/pubmed/18774732.
[144] "Insulin Resistance & Prediabetes | NIDDK." https://www.niddk.nih.gov/health-information/diabetes/overview/what-is-diabetes/prediabetes-insulin-resistance.
[145] "standards of medical care in diabetes—2017 - American ...." 6 Jan. 2017, https://professional.diabetes.org/files/media/dc_40_s1_final.pdf.

liver creating more liver fat as a vicious cycle. The fat enters the bloodstream as VLDL. The Islets of Langerhans of the pancreas readily receive the triglycerides causing a decrease in its response to high glucose levels causing more high blood sugar and more hyperinsulinemia in a vicious cycle in the liver and pancreas simultaneously.[146] Carbohydrates then are the major drivers predominantly creating visceral (belly) fat more than under the skin (subcutaneous) fat. QSS is then the key to reversal.

The body is a healing machine with all systems focused on homeostasis (balance) but system overloads cause multiple disruptions. Glucose overload causes damage through inflammation, oxidative stress, AGE's, and beta cell damage directly, which all affect beta cell function which causes more glucose overload creating a vicious cycle of damage. We focus on glucose but fructose (such as in high fructose corn syrup) overload leads to visceral fat which produces inflammatory substances

---

[146] "Putting insulin resistance into context by dietary reversal of type 2 ...." 2 Jun. 2017, https://www.rcpe.ac.uk/sites/default/files/jrcpe_47_2_taylor.pdf.

that damage the beta cells of the pancreas and leads to insulin resistance. This is not counting the damage to the alpha cells of the pancreas disrupting glucagon secretion which balances the actions of insulin. The systems are very complex and interdependent whereas the alpha cells have been found to protect the beta cells and transform themselves into new beta cells.[147]

The Islets of Langerhans also contains delta cells which produce somatostatin which can lower insulin secretion along with epsilon cells which produce ghrelin which is the hunger hormone that regulates weight and appetite. The focus again is on beta cell challenges which produce insulin but inflammation is the key feature regardless of subsequent pathology. Genes and environment (food, microbiome, physical activity, viruses, etc...) interact to create the conditions for inflammation to join in with either autoimmunity as in Type 1 and Type 1.5 (latent adult onset diabetes) and/or metabolic stress as in Type 2 diabetes. In addition, challenges to the gut microbiota causing gram negative bacteria to enter the

---

[147] "α-cell role in β-cell generation and regeneration - NCBI - NIH." https://www.ncbi.nlm.nih.gov/pmc/articles/PMC3442816/.

bloodstream leading to low grade inflammation can consequently cause insulin resistance and diabetes.[148] The big question though is why drugs became the focus for diabetes? Insulin is only one of the challenges of diabetes but all of the effort focuses on insulin in one way or another. We can understand seemingly complete beta cell destruction as in type 1 diabetes where there is no other choice, but for even the beginnings of latent adult onset diabetes (type 1.5) or definitely the early stages of type 2 diabetes, why are drugs the focus when drugs cannot reverse or solve the problem?

I worked for the Walgreen company for about 30 years in many areas but mainly as a pharmacist. For over 24 years, I taught herbal medicine and nutrition at Xavier's pharmacy school. A great mentor, Ed Poindexter opened the door for me to join a team of pharmacists whose mission was to train pharmacists to become diabetes educators. Troy Menard who succeeded him set everything up for me to travel to the company

---

[148] "Gut microbiome and type 2 diabetes: where we are and where ... - NCBI." 11 Oct. 2018, https://www.ncbi.nlm.nih.gov/pubmed/30366260.

headquarters in Deerfield Illinois along with about a dozen or so other pharmacists to be trained by the Joslin Diabetes team, who are truly a world renown research organization in diabetes care. We then brought the training to our respective regions. The entire training was based upon the DCCT (Diabetes Control and Complications Trial) and UKPDS (United Kingdom Prospective Diabetes Study) trials which showed that tight glucose control using drugs was the best method to reduce microvascular complications. Well being in retail for so long, it was great to go to Chicago to the main office and they gave us this cool bag which I still have today. Retail is patients/customers, fast paced and grueling. I love it because you really get to create relationships with patients and they are always excited to talk. The Xavier program had a nutrition component where I took 4th year students and trained them to educate our patients about nutrition in the pharmacy at the counseling window. Students only counseled patients and spent time backing up their recommendations with tons of research. We started in 1995 and the krebs cycle was our basis for understanding food metabolism, but around Hurricane Katrina (2005) the research exploded on visceral adiposity and changed everything, just as the microbiome is doing now. So while sitting in the Joslin training in Illinois, I kept thinking that this model would be perfect to train pharmacists around the country to educate patients about foods instead of drugs. There was and still is no team or organization that could do this the way Joslin had it set up since all of the focus was and still is mainly on drug therapy for diabetes.

Jude Pierre-Louis was the lead from Walgreens so after the training, I was ready to give him my 5 minute pitch. He loved it and asked me to present a proposal that he could bring to the big guys. I knew that I needed to compete with Joslin and other huge organizations, but they couldn't bring what we had at Xavier since we created it ourselves. Dr. Lanny Foss, who taught me pharmacognosy in school created the nutrition program. He was a life sciences chemist who wonderfully understood systems and curriculum so he brought together Dr. Albert Barrocas who was a big guy in ASPEN (American Society for Parenteral and Enteral Nutrition) along with Dr. Charles Jastram who was a part of that group also. He was a very detailed clinical pharmacist and runner. Dana Purdy, who worked for Dr. Barrocas as a dietician, also joined. She had a degree in chemistry and was way ahead of her time. This "A" team created an institutional course and a community course in the pharmacy school to take top students and bathe them in nutrition. Dr. Foss was a genius at developing new ideas and following through. We were using floppy disc drives with oral presentations and case studies which the students feared but did so well. This was drug people presenting about foods - same chemistry, the same biology, the same mechanisms of action but different types of research backing each area up.

Well the class and the Walgreen rotation would be the basis for bringing nutrition to the company. We had years of experience and systems to make it happen. Dana, Lanny and I were the community team. By this time though, Dana had passed away so of course Dr. Foss was the first person to call. We went to lunch at least twice a month for years discussing mainly the blending of nutrition and pharmacy. I had been doing a television program called Health Issues 2010, given to me by Dr. Keith C. Ferdinand when Katrina displaced him to Atlanta, where I would interview researchers, particularly in nutrition so I knew all of the players in New Orleans that could address this. My great friend who I interviewed at least 4 times was Dr. Lydia Bazzano. She is a true genius in understanding carbohydrates. She did the study on orange juice and diabetes and became famous with a low carb study that attracted major attention. She is currently 1 of 20 nationally recognized experts to serve on the 2020 Dietary Guidelines Advisory Committee. Next I called Dr. Liwei Chen from LSU who did research on the effects of sugar. Calynn Bunol, an excellent dietician came on board along with Dr. Maureen Shu, an immunologist who taught the basic nutrition course. Dr. Lanny Foss, who had accepted a position as dean of another pharmacy school, was always my go to person. Rounding out the team was Dr. Timothy Harlan from Tulane who was just beginning a program training physicians to educate patients about nutrition. He has since developed a wonderful program with the Goldring Center including a state of the art teaching kitchen that has truly advanced nutrition in medicine. We now had our dream team and a top proposal to change pharmacy the way anyone had known it, if Walgreens adopted it. We waited and waited with no answer. Finally, we found out that Walgreens committed to a huge deal with Johns Hopkins. The problem was that it would still be drugs, drugs and more drugs.

When trying to understand the effects diabetes has on the body, Katrina is the model. When the hurricane hit, I didn't evacuate with my wife and kids. I stayed behind to take care of my elderly parents and aunt. My sister closest to me had to stay since she was the deputy chief administrator for the city. She convinced me to stay at the Hyatt Hotel with my aunt and parents where the city set up space for needed government employees. I reluctantly agreed and drove them there with their wheelchairs into a nice room that Sunday night. As the storm picked up, windows popped out all over the huge hotel. By Monday afternoon, everything was peaceful except we couldn't return to the room, and there was little phone reception or food. By early Tuesday morning, my sister called and said we had to get out quickly and we could take her SUV. We loaded everyone in with wheelchairs and nothing else. People were asking if we could take them, but we had no room. The levees broke and the city was flooding fast. The SUV slowly made it through the rising floodwaters. Someone gave us directions to better streets so we slowly navigated through them and headed all the way to Houston. Thankfully, my parents and aunt lived through it. God kept us through the high water and the SUV didn't stop. However, the trauma led to the death of my mother a few months later, while my aunt and father died within a few years. The storm ripped the entire city apart. This is diabetes.

The sugar is a Katrina on the body creating damage. The body tries to repair and heal but another Katrina comes right back causing the blood vessels to inflame, beta cells to dysfunction, kidneys to fail and the heart to stop. Parts of the 9th ward still look like Katrina happened yesterday. Our family home was torn down. Sugar damages the gut microbiota, the eyes, brain and thoroughfares that allow nutrients to travel. We had trees everywhere on the streets blocking traffic with markers on houses as many thousands died on that day and the months and years after. Drugs couldn't stop Katrina. No man made system could have stopped Katrina. We have put all kinds of money to fix the levees but we just flooded because the pumps were broken. That's like drugs. It looks better but the sugar will overcome any defenses. Sodas and sweets - white bread, white rice and white pasta causes damage. Unlike Katrina we can halt those winds. Yes we can, but the same money and time spent on drug trials, delivery, education, systems and marketing could be spent on food trials, education, systems, marketing and delivery. But just as my wife and I tell each other when we complain: I'm doing the best I can. Drugs are it so let's look at them with a goal of getting off.

Diagnosis of diabetes is based upon having a fasting (> 8 hours) blood glucose level over 126 mg/dl or an

HbA1c over 6.5%. Prediabetes is diagnosed as a fasting blood glucose (FPG) of 100 mg/dl to 125 mg/dl or HbA1c from 5.7%-6.4%.[149]

The ADA's goal is to have an HbA1c under 7% now [150] with some targeted to 6.5% and others up to 8%. The DCCT (Diabetes Control and Complications Trial) advocated a goal of less than 6.05% for the intensive group who had to inject insulin 3 or more times a day, check blood sugar at least 4 times a day and visit the clinic monthly for an average of 6.5 years. Lower is better was the prevailing attitude for years after the DCCT in 1993 as most organizations advocated for a target of less than 6.5% because of it and the UKPDS. Then came the ACCORD trial in 1999. It had to be stopped early in 2008 because of a higher death rate in the intensive group which sought a goal of a <6%

---

[149] "2018 American Diabetes Association Standards of Care." https://diabetesed.net/wp-content/uploads/2017/12/2018-ADA-Standards-of-Care.pdf.

[150] "6. Glycemic Targets: Standards of Medical ...." http://care.diabetesjournals.org/content/41/Supplement_1/S55.

HbA1c.[151] More evidence came from The ADVANCE trial and the VADT studies.[152] Tight control did not reduce total or cardiovascular mortality. It did not reduce the risk of stroke. It did not reduce the risk of lower limb amputations. It may even increase the risk of heart failure. It did reduce the risk of non-fatal heart attacks (myocardial infarction). Those studies led to the relaxation of the target to 7% but as in cholesterol and hypertension, various organizations are advocating for even more relaxed targets. The American College of Physicians recommends an HbA1c below 8%.[153] Boussageon et al. describes a rationale for up to 9%.[154] Recently, the Endocrine Society recommended for those over 65 years of age, targets ranging from 7% to 8.5% depending upon the patient's overall health status

[151] "ACCORD Intensive Arm Stopped - Medscape." 6 Feb. 2008, https://www.medscape.com/viewarticle/569835.

[152] "Glycemic Targets in Diabetes Care: Emerging Clarity ... - NCBI - NIH." https://www.ncbi.nlm.nih.gov/pmc/articles/PMC4530694/.

[153] "American College of Physicians Recommending Controversial ...." 10 Mar. 2018, http://www.diabetesincontrol.com/american-college-of-physicians-recommending-controversial-increase-in-a1c-of-7-to-8/.

[154] "Prevention of complications in type 2 diabetes: is drug ... - NCBI - NIH." https://www.ncbi.nlm.nih.gov/pmc/articles/PMC5308113/.

and if they are at risk for hypoglycemia. This translates
into nighttime blood sugar readings of 90 to 250mg/dl
for those in poor health while also taking medications
that may cause hypoglycemia.[155]

The American Geriatrics Society recommends ranges
from 7% to 9% depending upon comorbidities and life
expectancy.[156]

The target is important because it determines at what
point a person should be medicated and if so, what drug
and at what dose. The target is not that important in
that type 2 diabetes is practically reversible. If the goal
is to continue to use medications to reduce
complications then targets matter greatly, but if the
goal is to reduce belly fat by quitting sodas and sweets,
switching to brown from white and sweating daily
(QSS), the beta cells will begin secreting insulin in
sufficient quantities again while the tissues would
become sensitive to the insulin again also. Even though

---

[155] "Treatment of Diabetes in Older Adults: An Endocrine ... -
Oxford Journals."
https://academic.oup.com/jcem/article/104/5/1520/5413486.
[156] "American Geriatrics Society | Choosing Wisely."
https://www.choosingwisely.org/societies/american-geriatrics-societ
y/.

the grocery stores and restaurants are full of obesogenic, sugar laden refined foods, we can choose to be well and do it.

Diabetes is deadly. As stated before, high blood sugar levels damage every cell in the body, so medication has to be taken when prescribed. Metformin will almost always be the first drug prescribed for type 2 diabetes. It causes stomach upset in 30% of users but it is one of the best drugs on the market because of its effectiveness. It lowers blood glucose through altering the intestinal microbiota, decreasing liver glucose production, increases glucose uptake by peripheral tissues, reduces liver fat production and accumulation and increases insulin sensitivity therefore reducing insulin resistance. Through these mechanisms the result is lower blood glucose levels, lower insulin levels, improved triglyceride levels[157] and a modest weight loss.[158] The mechanism of action of metformin is

---

[157] "Metformin lowers plasma triglycerides by promoting VLDL ... - NCBI." 22 Nov. 2013, https://www.ncbi.nlm.nih.gov/pubmed/24270984.
[158] "The Relationship between Frequently Used Glucose ... - NCBI - NIH." https://www.ncbi.nlm.nih.gov/pmc/articles/PMC5964532/.

complex and still not fully understood but regardless, the drug works. Metformin is actually derived from a natural product used in herbal medicine.[159] It was shown in 1918 that *Galega officinalis* (also known as goat's rue) lowered blood glucose. It is a traditional herbal medicine in Europe, found to be rich in guanidine which metformin is a derivative. It wasn't until 1998 that the long term cardiovascular benefits were identified by the UK Prospective Diabetes Study (UKPDS). This study provided a new rationale to begin using metformin as the initial drug for type 2 diabetes. During the 1940's it was discovered that it was effective against influenza.[160] Metformin is currently being rediscovered again because of its effects on the gut microbiome. Metformin has actions against tuberculosis, *Trichinella spiralis, Staphylococcus aureus, Pseudomonas aeruginosa,* hepatitis B virus, hepatitis C virus, and human immunodeficiency virus

---

[159] "The mechanisms of action of metformin - NCBI - NIH." 3 Aug. 2017, https://www.ncbi.nlm.nih.gov/pmc/articles/PMC5552828/.
[160] "The mechanisms of action of metformin - NCBI - NIH." 3 Aug. 2017, https://www.ncbi.nlm.nih.gov/pmc/articles/PMC5552828/.

(HIV).[161] The stomach upset challenges many patients but the benefits are substantial while being very inexpensive.

[161] "Is metformin poised for a second career as an ... - Wiley Online Library." 22 Dec. 2017, https://onlinelibrary.wiley.com/doi/full/10.1002/dmrr.2975.

Guidelines

Prediabetes: Guidelines actually suggest metformin to be considered for those with a BMI over 35 and under 60 years of age. Patient preference is critical in all new guidelines as therapy becomes more of a joint decision between patient and physician assessing risks and benefits which is why the team approach works best. If HbA1c is 1.5% above their target then the ADA suggests considering another drug to metformin. The key factor in the recommendations when choosing the next medication is their effect on weight. Insulin and sulfonylureas lead to weight gain because again insulin turns sugar into fat which is why many believe in the carbohydrate-insulin model as being the major driver of obesity where insulin is the key hormone. I believe it is much more complex with the carbohydrate-insulin interaction being a part of it but truly visceral adiposity and the gut microbiome mechanism may trump carb-insulin, let alone fructose metabolism in the liver. More studies will determine, but insulin leads to weight gain. When injected or taking pills to stimulate the pancreas to produce more, weight will increase as insulin increases. If the patient has ongoing weight loss and symptoms of high blood sugar are present then insulin may be recommended. Also if HbA1c is greater than 10% or blood sugar levels are over 300 mg/dl then insulin would be preferred since no other drug class can reduce blood sugars as well as insulin can. The team approach is critical here because this is where many patients resist treatment and give up. It is the needle. Many patients are terrified of needles. The discussions turn theological and/or fatalistic. Patients with support are much better able to adjust to this new lifestyle. For many, injections are more of a traumatic experience than surgery. The HbA1c targets themselves vary based upon patient support and resources along with the patient's attitude and expected effects of treatment. All of those factors are dominated by the beliefs and culture of the patient. Other factors that affect the HbA1c target are vascular complications, other diseases, life expectancy, disease duration, hypoglycemia and other adverse drug effects. The target is a major decision whose weight is shared by the patient.

For those under 10% and 1.5% above their target level, the next drug choice would be based upon if the patient also has artherosclerotic cardiovascular disease (ASCVD) which is the buildup of cholesterol plaque in arteries. Also of major concern is the drug's effect on heart failure, chronic kidney disease, low blood sugar risk, weight, cost, side effects and finding what the patient desires. If the patient doesn't buy into the treatment plan then it will be another one of those prescriptions that either doesn't get filled, not picked up or bottles that sit for months on the counter or in a drawer rarely used if at all.

SGLT-2 Inhibitors

Drugs are divided into groups or drug classes based on how they work (mechanism of action).

For most people over an 8% HbA1c and under 10% HbA1c, an SGLT2 inhibitor would be used after metformin because of the weight and cardiovascular benefits but lawsuits and/or side effects appear to be the reason they are not prescribed as much. After the FDA issued the black box (major) warning about amputations many doctors decreased or stopped prescribing Invokana (canagliflozin) or all of the SGLT2 inhibitors, possibly being not sure if it was a class effect or specific to that drug. The risk is relatively small at 0.6 events per 100 patient years, but also reduces CVD death by 0.5 events per patient years offsetting each other.[162] There are 1.7 million people taking SGLT2 inhibitors. The aggregate risk is low but that still led to 1370 amputations reported to the Vigibase database of

[162] "Some Physicians Switch Patients Off Invokana after ... - MedPage Today." 2 Sep. 2017, https://www.medpagetoday.com/primarycare/diabetes/67671.

adverse drug reactions for canagliflozin. That's compared to 51 amputations for empagliflozin and 28 for dapagliflozin.[163] Shared decision making is encouraged in all guidelines now, therefore any prescription for SGLT 2 inhibitors should initiate a discussion with the patient and if they desire, their family and spiritual advisor.

Other side effects include Fournier's gangrene, which the FDA issued warnings about, euglycemic diabetic ketoacidosis, acute kidney injury and hypotension. The benefits must be weighed against the risks. Patients on a strict very low carbohydrate diet (Keto) have a double problem[164] because not only are they at risk for diabetic ketoacidosis[165] because of reduced carbohydrate availability with fat oxidation leading to ketosis, but a keto diet leads to ketosis also, therefore doubling the risks.

[163] "Should All Patients with Type 2 Diabetes Mellitus and ... - NCBI." https://www.ncbi.nlm.nih.gov/pmc/articles/PMC6118832/.
[164] "Case report: Very low carbohydrate diet and SGLT-2-inhibitor ...." 8 Apr. 2019, https://www.reddit.com/r/ketoscience/comments/baum9y/case_report_very_low_carbohydrate_diet_and/. Accessed 8 Apr. 2019.
[165] "Euglycemic Diabetic Ketoacidosis: A Predictable ... - Diabetes Care." http://care.diabetesjournals.org/content/38/9/1638.

Empagliflozin (Jardiance), canagliflozin (Invokana), dapagliflozin (Farxiga) are the ones available now. They actually stop the glucose from being reabsorbed in the kidneys so it gets excreted (urinated) out. Sodium glucose transporter 2 (SGLT2) is the protein that moves the glucose from the pre-urine eventually back to the bloodstream. The liver is the chemical processing plant of the body and the kidneys are the filter of the body with SGLT2 being responsible for 90% of glucose being reabsorbed. SGLT1 is responsible for glucose being reabsorbed in the GI tract. An SGLT1 and SGLT2 combination inhibitor is being developed but only the SGLT2 inhibitors are available now which only can inhibit 50% of the glucose reabsorption.[166] [167] SGLT-2 inhibitors are a big challenge because of the rarity of side effects but those side effects are so major. There is a small HbA1C range for their use which makes the decision complex also. As in all drugs for type 2

---

[166] "Combined SGLT1 and SGLT2 Inhibitors and Their Role in ... - NCBI." https://www.ncbi.nlm.nih.gov/pubmed/29916741.
[167] "Physiology of renal glucose handling via SGLT1 ... - Springer Link." https://link.springer.com/article/10.1007/s00125-018-4656-5.

diabetes the challenge is assessing not only if this is the best treatment, but realizing that focusing on healthy eating changes everything. This must be done while also optimizing help from those who will support them on this journey. Other than lowering blood glucose concentrations, SGLT2 inhibitors have been found to have very positive effects in reducing hospitalization for heart failure and the progression of renal disease. For those with atherosclerotic cardiovascular disease, they have a moderate benefit in reducing major atherosclerotic cardiovascular events. The cardiology team will be looking at SGLT2 inhibitors because of these effects and it also adds to evidence that the endocrinology team should evaluate also.[168] [169] Quality nutrition is important at any age and disease progression, but remember that major organ damage drastically limits a physician's choice in medication

---

[168] "SGLT2 inhibitors for primary and secondary ... - The Lancet." 10 Nov. 2018, https://www.thelancet.com/journals/lancet/article/PIIS0140-6736(18)32590-X/fulltext.

[169] "European Society of Cardiology/Heart Failure Association ...." 9 Dec. 2019, https://onlinelibrary.wiley.com/doi/abs/10.1002/ejhf.1673.

reductions and greatly increases the complexity of deciding drug regimens. The key is to always communicate with the medical team because there is no way for a patient to know how valuable or important each drug is within the mix of medications. Teamwork makes the dream work always...

GLP-1 Receptor Agonists

The next class of drugs are the GLP-1 receptor agonists. They work by increasing GLP-1, an incretin in the gut which increases insulin secretion from the beta cells of the pancreas therefore reducing blood sugar. They also reduce glucagon secretion (which decreases blood sugar) from the alpha cells of the pancreas, delays gastric emptying time and decreases appetite directly (causing weight loss).[170] In response to food, incretins are released but in diabetics their release is diminished. Two thirds of the effects of insulin are thought to come from incretins. The power of this gut hormone highlights the importance of the gut region in body homeostasis. The beta cells of the pancreas sense blood glucose levels mainly based upon carbohydrate ingestion to adjust insulin levels. This occurs along with the gut sensing carbohydrate and fat presence thereby releasing the incretins, GIP and GLP-1, to affect insulin

---

[170] "Effects of GLP-1 on appetite and weight - NCBI - NIH." https://www.ncbi.nlm.nih.gov/pmc/articles/PMC4119845/.

release. The diminished release of incretins is thought to be a consequence of diabetes and not a cause.[171]

So GLP-1 receptor agonists enhance the actions of secreted GLP-1 from the gut while the other drugs we will discuss inhibit DPP-4 which inactivates GLP-1 quickly after its release. Both types of drugs end up allowing more of the incretins to reach the beta cells of the pancreas to release more insulin: DPP-4 antagonists and GLP-1 receptor agonists. DPP-4 antagonists can be taken as a tablet, but GLP-1 receptor agonists must be injected except for a tablet form that should be available soon.

GLP-1 RA's have a black box warning linking them to thyroid tumors in rodents but only one case has occurred in humans.[172]

Weight loss is a major feature of GLP-1 RA's since they have a direct effect on appetite while also delaying

[171] "The Incretin Approach for Diabetes Treatment | Diabetes."
http://diabetes.diabetesjournals.org/content/53/suppl_3/S197.
[172] "Review of head-to-head comparisons of glucagon-like ... - NCBI - NIH."
https://www.ncbi.nlm.nih.gov/pmc/articles/PMC5064617/.

gastric motility. They work on the gut and the brain together. They also increase resting energy expenditure which leads to some weight loss without added exercise. [173] An average weight loss of 6 pounds has been reported.[174]

- Dulaglutide (Trulicity), taken weekly
- Exenatide extended release (Bydureon), taken weekly
- Semaglutide (Ozempic), taken weekly
- Liraglutide (Victoza), taken daily
- Exenatide (Byetta), taken twice daily

The major issues with GLP-1 receptor agonists are gastrointestinal issues which cause the discontinuation of the drug at high rates. Nausea, vomiting and diarrhea are the problems with nausea being the worst, occurring in 4% to 51% of patients depending upon the

[173] "A clinical review of GLP-1 receptor agonists: efficacy and ... - NCBI - NIH." 9 Jul. 2015, https://www.ncbi.nlm.nih.gov/pmc/articles/PMC4509428/.
[174] "Effects of GLP-1 on appetite and weight - NCBI - NIH." https://www.ncbi.nlm.nih.gov/pmc/articles/PMC4119845/.

study, drug, dose and frequency.[175] Some physicians are prescribing ondansetron to be taken as needed to decrease the unbearable nausea when it occurs.

---

[175] "Adverse Effects of GLP-1 Receptor Agonists - NCBI." https://www.ncbi.nlm.nih.gov/pmc/articles/PMC5397288/.

DPP-4 Inhibitors

DPP-4 inhibitors have increased heart failure rates in clinical trials and observational studies.[176] They decrease hypertension and cholesterol levels but do not affect heart attack or stroke risks so obviously more studies are needed. Studies have shown small weight losses along with small weight gains to overall be designated as weight neutral.[177] The major concern about DPP-4 I's are the differences from GLP-1 RA's in negatively affecting heart failure even though both are incretin based therapies.[178] From Dr. Milton Packer of Baylor: "an increased risk of worsening heart failure appears to be a class effect of DPP-4 inhibitors, even in patients without a history of heart failure. DPP-4

[176] "Worsening Heart Failure During the Use of DPP-4 Inhibitors | JACC ...." 1 Mar. 2018, http://heartfailure.onlinejacc.org/content/early/2018/03/01/j.jchf.2017.12.016.

[177] "DPP-4 Inhibitors - Diabetes Care - American Diabetes Association." http://care.diabetesjournals.org/content/34/Supplement_2/S276.

[178] "GLP-1 receptor agonists and heart failure in diabetes. - NCBI." https://www.ncbi.nlm.nih.gov/pubmed/28431666.

inhibitors also cause a 75% increase in the risk of acute pancreatitis.[179]

DPP-4 inhibitors work just as GLP-1 RA's by increasing GLP-1 as DPP inactivates GLP-1, so by inhibiting the inactivator, it allows more GLP-1 to stimulate insulin release. This is what is amazing about pharmacology in that both classes of drugs have similar mechanisms of action but the effects and side effects are clearly different. DPP-4 inhibitors affect the strength of contraction of the heart muscle and enhances GLP 1's stimulus of cAMP (a messenger) in heart cells.[180] These actions may be a part of why each class of drugs have different effects on the heart. More study is needed but even though drugs are usually single chemical entities, tracing the exact way they will react in the complex human system is impossible since the variables are infinite. Imagine the possibilities with real food which

---

[179] "Incretin-based glucose-lowering medications and the risk of ...." 21 Nov. 2019, https://www.ncbi.nlm.nih.gov/pubmed/31750601.
[180] "Worsening Heart Failure During the Use of DPP-4 Inhibitors | JACC ...." 1 Mar. 2018, http://heartfailure.onlinejacc.org/content/early/2018/03/01/j.jchf.2017.12.016.

contain many chemical entities working synergistically to produce effects within the body.

Sulfonylureas

Sulfonylureas were the standard drugs used for many years and are still used in the 2nd generation form as glipizide, glyburide and glimepiride. 1.5 million cases of diabetes are diagnosed each year and 167 new drugs are in the pipeline. The potential is huge since the majority of patients are taking sulfonylureas or insulins with both causing hypoglycemia leading to falls, blackouts, car wrecks and more. GLP-1 RA's and DPP-4 I's both increase the actions of GLP-1 but neither stimulate its release. These differences in mechanisms are why hypoglycemia is a major concern in only certain classes of antidiabetic drugs with sulfonylureas being one of them.

Sulfonylureas directly stimulate the beta cells to release insulin whether food is present or not leading to the increased risk of low blood sugar. They also decrease the clearance of insulin in the liver. The challenge is that, as the constant stimulation of the beta cells to produce more insulin continues, this eventually leads to a faster failure of beta cell function. More insulin also causes weight gain. Insulin enhances the storage of fat (lipogenesis) and inhibits the mobilization of fat for energy in adipose tissues (lipolysis and free fatty acid oxidation).[181] This is the same reason many push for extremely low amounts of carbohydrates in the diet since carbohydrates predominantly, cause insulin release therefore weight gain. The issue isn't carbohydrates but refined carbohydrates. Whole grains have a favorable insulin response curve.[182] A group from Stanford should have results in 2020 from a 12 week study contrasting the ketogenic and the Mediterranean diets (whole grains) on HbA1c (diabetes).[183] The study period is much too short to provide any real visibility into the effects of whole grains on diabetes prevention or progression. Other differences in the diets would

[181] "Humulin R (regular, human insulin (rDNA origin)) dose … - PDR.net." https://www.pdr.net/drug-summary/Humulin-R-regular--human-insulin--rDNA-origin--2912.3423.

[182] "Effect of whole grains on insulin sensitivity in overweight …." https://academic.oup.com/ajcn/article/75/5/848/4689398.

[183] "Contrasting Ketogenic and Mediterranean Diets in … - ClinicalTrials.gov." https://clinicaltrials.gov/ct2/show/NCT03810378.

lead to infinite confounding variables but this is where high quality observational studies shine along with solid mechanisms of action. The evidence is clear that whole grains (carbs) are indeed healthy for diabetics and everyone else.

Serious hypoglycemic events are rare so therefore not a major issue in the use of sulfonylureas.[184] The issue is cardiovascular events. As in most side effects the question is how much risk should a person take. The relative risk is higher by 20% in mortality and by 13% in cardiovascular events compared to metformin[185] but for those who totally resist using the needle, the risks would be justified. Metformin is always the first choice after diet, but as a second drug this group offers an overall low risk choice. Normally if tolerated the GLP-1 RA's would be first but the nausea affects so many.

---

[184] "Physiological responses to hypoglycaemia – not all 'just in the ... - NCBI."
https://www.ncbi.nlm.nih.gov/pmc/articles/PMC2075345/.
[185] "Sulfonylureas and the Risks of Cardiovascular Events ... - Diabetes Care." http://care.diabetesjournals.org/content/40/5/706.

TZD

Thiazolidinediones include pioglitazone (Actos) and
rosiglitazone (Avandia). Heart Failure is the major
concern and is contraindicated in those with Class III
and Class IV heart failure. The warning is that the drug
can cause or exacerbate congestive heart failure in some
patients. DeFronzo et al. argues that the benefits
outweigh the risks since the number of patients in the
IRIS study who developed heart failure was similar
between pioglitazone and placebo. Also if any edema is
present the dosage can be adjusted. The edema results
primarily from vasodilation, with renal sodium
retention being secondary to the peripheral
vasodilation. What is interesting is that even with the
renal sodium retention, blood pressure declines, there
is no effect on left ventricular function of the heart and
pioglitazone improves diastolic dysfunction.
Pioglitazone has a number of benefits including
reduced cardiovascular events, retarding the
atherosclerotic process, a potent insulin sensitizer,

preserves beta cell function, and improves
NAFLD/nonalcoholic steatohepatitis.

Pioglitazone causes weight gain by stimulating appetite
by stimulating PPARy receptors in the hypothalamus. It
also increases fat cell creation but it appears to fill the
cells with fat from the arterial walls therefore increasing
survival.[186]

Rosiglitazone suffered a different fate being implicated
in increasing cardiovascular events which led the FDA
to place prescribing restrictions on doctors therefore
decreasing sales from $3 billion to $9 million. It has
since been cleared after the FDA reviewed the study
again but sales have not rebounded.[187] Pioglitazone's
sales suffered from this fallout also while it appears that
the benefits and side effects involved are a class effect.
Arnold et al. expressed concerns about 25% to 40% of
pioglitazone patients having evidence of heart failure
while also concerns of heart failure and TZDs being

---

[186] "Pioglitazone: The forgotten, cost-effective ... - SAGE Journals."
https://journals.sagepub.com/doi/10.1177/1479164118825376.
[187] "GSK's Avandia is free and clear at the FDA, 8 years after
heart-safety ...." 17 Dec. 2015,
https://www.fiercepharma.com/pharma/gsk-s-avandia-free-and-
clear-at-fda-8-years-after-heart-safety-controversy-began.

"under-recognized".[188] It would be expected that clearer guidance would be available on such an important drug but with pioglitazone being a generic drug, funding for marketing to physicians isn't available. With 2.5 million academic papers published each year and drug sales nearing a trillion dollars each year, we have a problem. What makes thiazolidinediones so special is the novel mechanism of action in which they bind to the PPARγ receptors in adipocytes to promote fat cell creation, increasing fatty acid uptake with fat that was found to be from arterial cell walls. The location of the adipocytes are in the periphery and not visceral fat which therefore cause a reduction in the liver and muscles of circulating fatty acid concentrations and lipid availability.[189] Insulin resistance is the mechanism by which diabetes causes damage and TZDs improve patient's sensitivity to insulin so there could not be a better drug fundamentally. The heart failure concerns

[188] "Pioglitazone: The forgotten, cost-effective ... - SAGE Journals." https://journals.sagepub.com/doi/10.1177/1479164118825376..
[189] "Thiazolidinediones - mechanisms of action - NPS MedicineWise." https://www.nps.org.au/australian-prescriber/articles/thiazolidinediones-mechanisms-of-action.

should be placed in this context. Of course QSS is truly the answer but as far as drugs go, this one has always been encouraging.

Insulin

Insulins haven't truly changed in years. More gadgets
and options now but still the same idea of an injection
under the skin with a concern for blood sugar going too
low with the biggest issue there being falling down
stairs, car wrecks and other accidents. Type 1's are
mainly younger and more experienced and in fact very,
very experienced so they know what to do. They still
may not do it but they know. Imagine a 14 year old kid
in grade school wanting to be like everyone else. A neat
inhaled insulin is available but the drug has minimal
exposure. Many insurance companies are not paying for
it without a long prior authorization process and there
is no real sales team greeting physicians and
pharmacists. They're using television, but so far the
world uses the needle as it has since it was discovered
by Dr. Banting and Charles Best in 1921. It is still the
best drug for uncontrolled diabetes with only low blood
sugar and weight gain as major side effects. It is
necessary for HBA1c's over 9% - 10% along with blood

sugar spikes. GLP-1 RA's HbA1c lowering ability ranges from 0.78% to 1.9% which pales in comparison to insulin. Also three trials attempted to compare GLP-1 RA's to prandial insulin with poor results. The high side effect profile, particularly the nausea, vomiting and diarrhea of GLP-1 RA's also challenge many.[190] Insulin works well with the main side effects being weight gain and hypoglycemia. The do-it-yourself crowd devised a system combining an insulin pump and a continuous glucose monitor to automate the delivery of insulin based upon blood glucose levels, drastically reducing the amount of hypoglycemic episodes. It's really DIY and not realistic for most people now, but the future looks bright for these artificial pancreas systems.[191] [192]

---

[190] "GLP-1 Receptor Agonists: An Alternative for Rapid-Acting Insulin?." 14 Oct. 2016, https://www.uspharmacist.com/article/GLP-1-receptor-agonists-an-alternative-for-rapidacting-insulin.

[191] "'Looping' Created an Underground Insulin-Pump Market - The Atlantic." 29 Apr. 2019, https://www.theatlantic.com/science/archive/2019/04/looping-created-insulin-pump-underground-market/588091/.

[192] "OpenAPS." https://openaps.org/.

An adhesive patch, the size of a quarter that monitors glucose and delivers insulin is being tested. This would be an ideal artificial pancreas system if it works.[193] Weight gain is the next big hurdle but in comparison to possible side effects of the other drug classes, it is a wise decision where necessary. The goal for type 2 diabetics is to reduce their blood sugar and HbA1c to eliminate insulin. Once on QSS, blood sugar can drop quickly depending upon previous diet therefore testing is of the utmost importance. The continuous glucose monitor systems are excellent and also allowing for a new proposed metric called TIR, time in range, which gives the amount of time a patient stays between 70mg/dl and 180mg/dl.[194] It will be a useful tool, but just as glycemic index/load has flaws, time in range is limited in its recognition of the effects of fructose which doesn't affect blood sugar as much, but does affect belly fat and

---

[193] "This coin-sized smart insulin patch could monitor glucose for ...." 5 Feb. 2020,
https://www.medicaldesignandoutsourcing.com/this-coin-sized-smart-insulin-patch-could-monitor-glucose-for-diabetes-management/.
Accessed 15 Feb. 2020.
[194] "Metrics Beyond Hemoglobin A1C in Diabetes Management ... - NCBI." 1 May. 2017,
https://www.ncbi.nlm.nih.gov/pmc/articles/PMC5444503/.

insulin resistance. TIR is perfect in gauging the effects of various foods on blood sugar but is a poor indicator of the frequency or severity of hypoglycemia.[195] Overall it will be great but as in everything in context. The goal is reversal for type 2's with eating and exercise.

---

[195] "Positioning time in range in diabetes management - Springer ...." https://link.springer.com/article/10.1007/s00125-019-05027-0.

Category/Name of Insulin	Brand Name (manufacturer)	Preparation(s)
Rapid-Acting		
Insulin Lispro	Humalog (Lilly)	Vial, cartridge, disposable pen
Insulin Aspart	Novolog (Novo Nordisk)	Vial, cartridge, disposable pen
Insulin Glulisine	Apidra (Sanofi-Aventis)	Vial, disposable pen
Technosphere insulin	Afrezza	Inhaler
Short-Acting		
Regular Human	Humulin R (Lilly) Novolin R (Novo Nordisk)	Vial
Intermediate-Acting		
NPH Human	Humulin N (Lilly) Novolin N (Novo Nordisk)	Vial, disposable pen Vial
Long-Acting		
Insulin Detemir	Levemir (Novo Nordisk)	Vial, disposable pen

Insulin Glargine	Lantus (Sanofi-Aventis) Basaglar (Lilly) Toujeo (Sanofi-Aventis)	Vial, cartridge, disposable pen Basaglar is only available as a disposable pen Toujeo is only available as a disposable pen
Insulin Degludec	Tresiba (Novo Nordisk)	Disposable pen

Insulin Mixtures

NPH/Regular (70%/30%)	Humulin 70/30 (Lilly) Novolin 70/30 (Novo Nordisk)	Vial, disposable pen Vial
Protamine/Lispro (50%/50%)	Humalog Mix 50/50(Lilly)	Vial, disposable pen
Protamine/Lispro (75%25%)	Humalog Mix 75/25(Lilly)	Vial, disposable pen
Protamine/Aspart (70/30)	Novolog Mix 70/30 (Novo Nordisk)	Vial, disposable pen

Insulin	Onset (hr.)	Peak (hr.)	Duration (hr.)	Appearance
Fast-acting Insulin Aspart	Within 5 min	~1	3-4	Clear
Insulin Lispro	within 15 min	~ 1	3-5	Clear
Insulin Aspart	within 15 min	1-3	3-5	Clear
Insulin Glulisine	0.25-0.5	0.5-1	4	Clear
Technosphere	within 5 min	15 min	about 3	Powder
Regular	~ 1	2-4	5-8	Clear
NPH	1-2	4-10	14+	Cloudy
Insulin Detemir	3-4	6-8 (though relatively flat)	up to 20-24	Clear
Insulin Glargine	1.5	Flat	24	Clear
Insulin Degludec	1	9	42	Clear
Lispro Mix 50/50	0.25-0.5	0.5-3	14-24	Cloudy
Lispro Mix 75/25	0.25-5	0.5-2.5	14-24	Cloudy

Drug Class	Rx's	Market Share
Metformin	81,305,415	41.08%
Insulin	57,583,955	29.10%
SU	33,908,286	17.13%
DPP-4 I	12,223,830	6.18%
TZD	6,563,097	3.32%
GLP-1 RA	3,225,863	1.63%
SGLT-2 I	3,102,040	1.57%

Class	Examples	Weight Effects	Heart Effects	Side Effects	Pill /Injection
SGLT2 inhibitors	Invokana, Farxiga, Jardiance	weight loss	better	Ampu-tations **(major warning)** and bone fracture risks with Invokana	pill
GLP-1 receptor agonist	Bydureon, Victoza, Trulicity	weight loss	better (Victoza)	Thyroid C-cell tumor risks **(major warning)**, stomach upset	injection
DPP-4 inhibitors	Januvia, Tradjenta, Onglyza	none	worse (Onglyza)	Acute pancrea-titis, joint pain	pill
Thiazolidinediones	Pioglitazone	weight gain	Increased risk	Congestive heart failure **(major warning)**, bone fracture, bladder cancer	pill

Sulfonylureas (2nd generation)	Glimepiride, glipizide, glyburide	weight gain	none	Increased risk of cardio-vascular mortality	pill
Insulin	Lantus, Humalog, Novolog, NPH	weight gain	none	low blood sugar	injection

Calories Burned

in 30-minute activities[196]

Gym Activities	125-lb person	155-lb person
Weight Lifting: general	90	112
Aerobics: water	120	149
Stretching, Hatha Yoga	120	149
Calisthenics: moderate	135	167
Riders: general	150	186
Aerobics: low impact	165	205
Stair Step Machine: general	180	223
Teaching aerobics	180	223

---

[196] "Calories burned in 30 minutes for people of three ... - Harvard Health." 13 Aug. 2018, https://www.health.harvard.edu/diet-and-weight-loss/calories-burned-in-30-minutes-of-leisure-and-routine-activities. 31 Dec. 2018.

Weight Lifting: vigorous	180	223
Aerobics, Step: low impact	210	260
Aerobics: high impact	210	260
Bicycling, Stationary: moderate	210	260
Rowing, Stationary: moderate	210	260
Calisthenics: vigorous	240	298
Circuit Training: general	240	298
Rowing, Stationary: vigorous	255	316
Elliptical Trainer: general	270	335
Ski Machine: general	285	353
Aerobics, Step: high impact	300	372
Bicycling, Stationary: vigorous	315	391

Training and Sport Activities

Billiards	75	93
Bowling	90	112
Dancing: slow, waltz, foxtrot	90	112
Frisbee	90	112
Volleyball: non-competitive, general play	90	112
Water Volleyball	90	112
Archery: non-hunting	105	130
Golf: using cart	105	130
Hang Gliding	105	130
Curling	120	149
Gymnastics: general	120	149
Horseback Riding: general	120	149

Tai Chi	120	149
Volleyball: competitive, gymnasium play	120	149
Walking: 3.5 mph (17 min/mi)	120	149
Badminton: general	135	167
Walking: 4 mph (15 min/mi)	135	167
Kayaking	150	186
Skateboarding	150	186
Snorkeling	150	186
Softball: general play	150	186
Walking: 4.5 mph (13 min/mi)	150	186
Whitewater: rafting, kayaking	150	186
Dancing: disco, ballroom, square	165	205

Golf: carrying clubs	165	205
Dancing: Fast, ballet, twist	180	223
Fencing	180	223
Hiking: cross-country	180	223
Skiing: downhill	180	223
Swimming: general	180	223
Walk/Jog: jog <10 min.	180	223
Water Skiing	180	223
Wrestling	180	223
Basketball: wheelchair	195	242
Race Walking	195	242
Ice Skating: general	210	260
Racquetball: casual, general	210	260

Rollerblade Skating	210	260
Scuba or skin diving	210	260
Sledding, luge, toboggan	210	260
Soccer: general	210	260
Tennis: general	210	260
Basketball: playing a game	240	298
Bicycling: 12-13.9 mph	240	298
Football: touch, flag, general	240	298
Hockey: field & ice	240	298
Rock Climbing: rappelling	240	298
Running: 5 mph (12 min/mile)	240	298
Running: pushing wheelchair, marathon wheeling	240	298
Skiing: cross-country	240	298

Snow Shoeing	240	298
Swimming: backstroke	240	298
Volleyball: beach	240	298
Bicycling: BMX or mountain	255	316
Boxing: sparring	270	335
Football: competitive	270	335
Orienteering	270	335
Running: 5.2 mph (11.5 min/mile)	270	335
Running: cross-country	270	335
Bicycling: 14-15.9 mph	300	372
Martial Arts: judo, karate, kickbox	300	372
Racquetball: competitive	300	372

Rope Jumping	300	372
Running: 6 mph (10 min/mile)	300	372
Swimming: breaststroke	300	372
Swimming: laps, vigorous	300	372
Swimming: treading, vigorous	300	372
Water Polo	300	372
Rock Climbing: ascending	330	409
Running: 6.7 mph (9 min/mile)	330	409
Swimming: butterfly	330	409
Swimming: crawl	330	409
Bicycling: 16-19 mph	360	446
Handball: general	360	446
Running: 7.5 mph (8 min/mile)	375	465

Running: 8.6 mph (7 min/mile)	435	539
Bicycling: > 20 mph	495	614
Running: 10 mph (6 min/mile)	495	614

Outdoor Activities

Planting seedlings, shrubs	120	149
Raking Lawn	120	149
Sacking grass or leaves	120	149
Gardening: general	135	167
Mowing Lawn: push, power	135	167
Operate Snow Blower: walking	135	167
Plant trees	135	167
Gardening: weeding	139	172

Carrying & stacking wood	150	186
Digging, spading dirt	150	186
Laying sod / crushed rock	150	186
Mowing Lawn: push, hand	165	205
Chopping & splitting wood	180	223
Shoveling Snow: by hand	180	223

Home & Daily Life Activities

Sleeping	19	23
Watching TV	23	28
Reading: sitting	34	42
Standing in line	38	47
Cooking	75	93

Child-care: bathing, feeding, etc.	105	130
Food Shopping: with cart	105	130
Moving: unpacking	105	130
Playing w/kids: moderate effort	120	149
Heavy Cleaning: wash car, windows	135	167
Child games: hopscotch, jacks, etc.	150	186
Playing w/kids: vigorous effort	150	186
Moving: household furniture	180	223
Moving: carrying boxes	210	260

Home Repair

Auto Repair	90	112

Wiring and Plumbing	90	112
Carpentry: refinish furniture	135	167
Lay or remove carpet/tile	135	167
Paint, paper, remodel: inside	135	167
Cleaning rain gutters	150	186
Hanging storm windows	150	186
Paint house: outside	150	186
Carpentry: outside	180	223
Roofing	180	223

Occupational Activities

Computer Work	41	51
Light Office Work	45	56

Sitting in Meetings	49	60
Desk Work	53	65
Sitting in Class	53	65
Truck Driving: sitting	60	74
Bartending/Server	75	93
Heavy Equip. Operator	75	93
Police Officer	75	93
Theater Work	90	112
Welding	90	112
Carpentry Work	105	130
Coaching Sports	120	149
Masseur, standing	120	149
Construction, general	165	205

Coal Mining	180	223
Horse Grooming	180	223
Masonry	210	260
Forestry, general	240	298
Heavy Tools, not power	240	298
Steel Mill: general	240	298
Firefighting	360	446

The Team Approach

The Doctor, Pastor, Family Team

Doctors and pastors normally interact at the time of death, but to patients with a pastor (PWP), that pastor has the greatest influence on the motivation, behavior, and emotional well-being of that patient. The pastor-member relationship can be stronger than family relationships and much stronger than that of the medical team-patient relationship. Pastors may see members twice weekly for many years, counsel, work on teams with, marry, funeralize family members, baptize, christen children and more... The doctor is requesting patients to make life changes but the pastor is usually best able to encourage, motivate, and inspire those changes. In fact the only person that by profession is dedicated to improving the entire life of that patient is the pastor. This is the uniqueness of the pastor-member relationship. Family may or may not be able to or care to help. In fact, generational trauma, toxic relationships and abuse within families contribute greatly to personal dysfunction. The medical team, while dedicated to the physical and mental care of the patient is not able to address the inner concerns of faith and philosophy. The team approach is the optimum way to address the health and wellness of patients.

The move to encourage the medical team to improve spiritual health is truly ill advised. Just as a pastor is usually not trained to address medication and surgery questions, doctors are not trained in doctrinal/philosophical issues of their patients. Religious/doctrinal beliefs vary within a church, within denominations, and between religions, so for the medical professionals to even attempt to navigate those waters is unwise. The only way it can work is in faith environments where the medical professionals publicize their beliefs and are allowed to be questioned about them. Then a patient may choose to allow the medical professional to enter into that philosophical realm with the patient. The key is the patient having a voluntary choice that is patient initiated. Also the belief system and doctrines of the provider should be well publicized with financial and religious conflicts of interest disclosed. An example would be a religious hospital where the belief system of the staff is posted on their website and the staff is available to discuss those beliefs. The patient can expect a religious environment regardless of their beliefs, but a religious conversation should still be patient initiated because the power differential between doctor and patient is too great. By definition, religions are seeking adherents for various reasons therefore it is disingenuous to believe a professional can be unbiased. For a physician to give spiritual advice, prayer or offer scriptures may very well go totally against what the patient's pastor is teaching and can be spiritually destructive and therefore emotionally and consequently physically damaging to the patient. Free will of the patient is a right therefore the patient has full authority to decide if they choose to receive spiritual advice from a physician, pharmacist, nurse or anyone if the patient desires. If a patient does not have the free will to receive the spiritual advice that they desire, the relationship should be investigated. The religion could be a dangerous cult. 70% of atheists believe churches have too much influence in society so they'll think all religions are cultish, therefore balance is key.[197] Transparency, freedom, fairness and respect should dominate the relationships.

What happened to western medicine since the advent of the industrial age is a disdain for spirituality altogether. This has left patients separated from their most powerful motivating force - their pastor. This leaves doctors separated from their most valuable team member in effecting behavioral change - the patient's pastor. It's time to bring this star player on the team. The pastor is carrying a bazooka while the physician has a slingshot in effecting behavioral change. The pastor gets maybe 100 shots a year , while the physician may get 3 to 4 shots a year with a pea shooter: scientific facts. The pastor is speaking with the force of God Himself while the doctor is using clinical studies, which to the patient, changes with the wind. The patient's free will decides, but if both can work together on the same team, then we can have true wellness.

---

[197] "10 facts about atheists | Pew Research Center." 6 Dec. 2019, https://www.pewresearch.org/fact-tank/2019/12/06/10-facts-about-atheists/.

Historical Context: Theo/Pharma/Nutrition

Medicine has only recently begun to understand the value of nutrition and social connections. Nutrition was seen as a form of alternative medicine. The health system didn't have to enter the "lifestyle" of the patient, but just give directions and expect compliance whether it be food types and portions or medication adherence or to have surgery. The doctor gave the order and the patient was to follow or else be called non-compliant with penalties. I regularly speak to patients who discuss how their physician would get angry at them if they didn't lose weight or take their medications as prescribed. With a better understanding of the body, medicine is now dependent upon the patient to "believe" their messages. Patients now get angry at doctors. With most of them being employees and paid by huge insurance plans, their status has shrunk in the public's eye. Patients have access to all information and are using it to upset quiet doctor's offices as the tables have turned. Respected, yes but a big power shift is occurring.[198]

Christianity has never left medicine but medicine totally left Christianity. Jesus taught extensively about healing and spirituality. The concept of mind, body and spirit is central to Christianity. Luke was a physician who specialized in herbal prescriptions while Jesus focused on healing using mud, spit, words, etc. through spiritual power. They worked together without any conflict, with the separate approaches blending well together.

Hippocrates is credited with separating medicine from religion and/or philosophy around 400 BC so Luke may have been training through that approach. Hippocrates was a principal author of the Corpus Hippocraticum which gives background to the type of medicine Luke may have been trained to practice. Greek philosophy

---

[198] "Connecting With Patients-The Missing Links. - NCBI." https://www.ncbi.nlm.nih.gov/pubmed/31910264.

was very strong. Greece did not fall to the Romans until 146 BC, but while the Romans did conquer the Greeks, it is said that the Greeks actually conquered the Romans because of the dominance of Greek language, art, architecture, philosophy and intellect which included medicine. It was Horace who said, *Graecia capta ferum victorem cepit* ("Captive Greece captured her rude conqueror"). The Greeks who had incorporated Egyptian ideas and remedies dating back to Imhotep in 2600 BC[199] [200] transformed medical care in their use of logic and reasoning. Their influence lasted through the Roman period until today where most medical schools still use some form of the Hippocratic oath. The original version is:

Hippocratic Oath

I swear by Apollo Physician and Asclepius and Hygieia and

Panaceia and all the gods and goddesses, making them my

---

[199] "Greek medicine: a new look | Brain | Oxford Academic - Oxford Journals." 16 May. 2016,
[200]

witnesses, that I will fulfil according to my ability and judgment this oath and this covenant:

To hold him who has taught me this art as equal to my parents and to live my life in partnership with him, and if he is in need of money to give him a share of mine, and to regard his offspring as equal to my brothers in male lineage and to teach them this art - if they desire to learn it - without fee and covenant; to give a share of precepts and oral instruction and all the other learning to my sons and to the sons of him who has instructed me and to pupils who have signed the covenant and have taken an oath according to the medical law, but no one else.

I will apply dietetic measures for the benefit of the sick according to my ability and judgment; I will keep them from harm and injustice. I will neither give a deadly drug to anybody who asked for it, nor will I make a suggestion to this effect. Similarly I will not give to a woman an abortive remedy. In purity and holiness I will guard my life and my art.

I will not use the knife, not even on sufferers from stone, but will

withdraw in favor of such men as are engaged in this work.

Whatever houses I may visit, I will come for the benefit of the sick,

remaining free of all intentional injustice, of all mischief and in

particular of sexual relations with both female and male persons,

be they free or slaves.

What I may see or hear in the course of the treatment or even

outside of the treatment in regard to the life of men, which on no

account one must spread abroad, I will keep to myself, holding

such things shameful to be spoken about.

If I fulfil this oath and do not violate it, may it be granted to me to

enjoy life and art, being honored with fame among all men for all

time to come; if I transgress it and swear falsely, may the opposite

of all this be my lot.

Luke was a physician as Paul was a tent builder. Luke was probably Greek while Paul was a Roman citizen. We know he was a Gentile whose name was from Greek origin. His language and writing style illustrates his high level of education.[201] So Luke probably was educated in the Hippocrates tradition but was able to transform its use to truly help people: balance.

Reflective of his medical training Luke begins his account of Jesus' life as an "accurate" account to Theophilus. The context was that there were many other accounts being circulated and his was to bring order so we could be certain of the truth. Luke's writing begins with the birth of John the Baptist through the preaching of the gospel at the capital of the Roman empire and ending with the book of Acts. He was with Paul from his second missionary journey until the end of his life except for six years when Paul left Luke to tend to the new church at Philippi. At the end of his life, Paul told Timothy to come quickly because "only Luke is with me". Everyone else was gone. It was Luke, the physician who was a loyal, hard working believer who also wrote a third of the New Testament as Paul also

---

[201] "Luke: Physician and Historian - Grace to You." 8 Nov. 1998, https://www.gty.org/library/sermons-library/42-1/luke-physician-and-historian.

wrote a third. He was the epitome of reason and skill, being filled with supernatural power. He understood false teachings and their threat to truth. As Hippocrates' goal was to bring order within the medical world, Luke's goal was to bring order in the historical and spiritual worlds. In Luke's gospel he wrote of a woman who had spent all of her money on physicians but no one was able to heal her. She touched the hem of His garment and immediately her faith made her well. The word "well" is from the Greek word "sozo" meaning saved, or whole. She was physically healed, mentally healed and spiritually healed, so Luke was able to transverse both worlds comfortably being an expert at both. Luke's life and work is the model for understanding how medicine and spirituality should work together to bring healing, peace, wellness, nourishing relationships and joy. The Jesus/Luke relationship was the doctor/pastor relationship to model.

Historical Background

To truly understand the current doctor/pastor relationship we need to look back at history to see how we arrived at this point. Looking at the past totally illuminates the present. First we looked at the relationship during Luke and Jesus' time. Next we'll look at Abraham's time then the European church, then we'll review the church in Africa from a historical perspective to the present..

As stated, Greek culture borrowed much from the Egyptians who were able to construct pyramids by the 3rd millennium BC (before Christ). Agriculture dates before the 10th millennium BC with Egypt and Mesopotamia having advanced systems by the 4th millennium BC also while trading with each other. Abraham left Mesopotamia (Ur) around 800 years after the 1st pyramid was built. The first written records of herbal preparations are from Mesopotamian clay tablet writings during the reign of King Assurbanipal around the time of Abraham's departure to Palestine. It was the first known materia medica which contained 250 products which included garlic. So Abraham travelled from Mesopotamia to Palestine to Egypt and back to Palestine. All of these were areas of very advanced civilizations. He or his family may have been part of a scribal school in Ur, and/or farmers of fruits, grains and vegetables. They may have seen many constructed pyramids or studied law codes. In Egypt, medicine and mathematics reached its climax during Abraham's lifetime as it was a glorious time in human history. There were buildings, city/states, accounting practices, professions and more. Medical practices and herbal medicine were a normal part of life. Herbal medicine and vegetables cannot be separated. It was also impossible to separate beliefs from the environment from behavior as it is today.

European Church History

The early church continued as Luke described in the book of Acts ministering to the total man.

In Europe the Roman emperor Constantine greatly expanded the Christian church in 313 AD with the Edict of Milan fostering the benevolent treatment of Christians who had before been killed, persecuted and crucified for their faith.

1200 years later Martin Luther nailed the 95 Theses to the Wittenberg Castle church door protesting the abuses of the Catholic Church whose doctrine included exorcisms, miracles, faith healing, but the protest was mainly because the church sold indulgences which provided a financial way to avoid purgatorial fire for those who could afford it. Martin Luther's protest led to the Protestant Reformation which was the most significant change since Constantine's policies. This led to the abolishing of the sale of indulgences but also an anti-Catholic sentiment that abolished healing and miracles within the Protestant churches. Even though others protested before, Martin Luther's protest had the aide of the printing press which was invented a century earlier. John Wycliff who translated the Bible into English, began a major protest but was imprisoned. Known as the second reformer, John Hus was burned at the stake but with the invention of the Gutenberg Printing Press, Martin Luther's Protestant Reformation was on fire. A single press might produce 3600 pages a day while a monk might have copied four or five. The Catholic Church instituted a Counter-Reformation in response that included ecclesiastical reconfiguration, a series of wars, anti-corruption efforts, training of priests, and new spiritual movements focusing on a personal relationship with Christ. The church repositioned itself.

The Protestants split between the Magisterial Reformation and the Radical Reformation which divisions developed that were as or more violent than the Catholic-Protestant hostilities. The church violence was indicative of the broader violence it fostered throughout the world. The Protestant Reformation occurred at the same time as Europe's church driven genocidal conquest of Africa and the Americas. Columbus entered America in 1492 where immediately after that the Catholic church issued a series of public decrees from the pope (papal bulls) to organize the colonizing enterprise.[202] Throughout the conquests around the world, the church and state worked closely together. In some areas like Australia and North America where settlers needed their land to live, the people were exterminated. Where they mainly wanted wealth and needed the people to work that land, the church and government together set up a scam system called a trustee system. The settler would teach the real landowners the basics of the Christian faith in exchange they would work for the settler and sign documents validating the agreement but which included obedience to the king and the pope. When they failed it provided a legal excuse for taking their land, death and/or

---

[202] "Church History: An Essential Guide - Justo L. González - Google Books."
https://books.google.com/books/about/Church_History.html?id=43akRKSPWZ0C.

enslavement. These and other methods were used throughout the European conquests of much of the world. Missions were the arm of the colonial power.

This was part of the European side of the story. The view from Africa offers an entirely different perspective. So leaving from Luke to the present, the African side offers a different view of church history. Luke participated in bringing the gospel to Asia and Europe but Mark brought the gospel to Egypt.

African Church History

Africa was as much a home to Christianity as anywhere else. Luke was a physician who traveled with Paul, but Mark brought Christianity to Egypt. There are reports that possibly Barnabas brought Christianity to Egypt along with Mark after they split from Paul in a vigorous argument in which Paul challenged Mark's maturity. The New Testament doesn't discuss missionary journeys to Egypt but there was a sizable community of Jews in Egypt during that period with many indications of missionary work there. Luke's focus was on Paul's missionary journeys while the other 12 apostles certainly evangelized. Paul would not tread on another's territory as he said and particularly Barnabas's. The Alexandrian, Apollos was further educated by the husband and wife team, Aquila and Pricilla illustrating an underdeveloped doctrine within Egypt maybe concerning Pentecost, women in ministry or infant baptism, but nonetheless accurate Christianity. Alexandria was the greatest port of the eastern

Meditarranean.[203] The evidence is overwhelming, demonstrating a Christian presence in Africa from the earliest periods of the church. The three major Christian people groups were the Egyptians, the Ethiopians and the Nubians. The Ethiopian church and the Egyptian Coptic church exists until this day.

In Egypt, the Copts were an ancient Hamitic people who practiced the religion of the Pharaohs prior to the bible writer Mark having established the church there. It was established according to Coptic tradition.[204] Mark's evangelism would place Africa as containing one of the earliest churches outside of Jerusalem.[205] Egypt was home to over 200,000 Jews, many already there from the Babylonian and Assyrian exiles, who would have been fertile ground for evangelising. They were first exiled from Egypt to Canaan through Moses but

---

[203] "The Association of Mark and Barnabas with Egyptian Christianity (Part ....."
https://biblicalstudies.org.uk/pdf/eq/1982-4_219.pdf.
[204] "(PDF) Christianity in Africa: a historical appraisal - ResearchGate."
https://www.researchgate.net/publication/269965860_Christianity_in_Africa_a_historical_appraisal..
[205] CHANCELLOR, WILLIAMS. DESTRUCTION OF BLACK CIVILIZATION: Great Issues of a Race from 4500 B.c. to 2000 A.d. WWW BNPUBLISHING COM

now exiled to Egypt among other places. The Christians then would be bringing the gospel to Jews as well as Copts, other Egyptians and Greeks who had conquered Egypt from the Persians who also conquered the Jews during the reign of Darius. The Greeks were deeply polythiestic with many gods, goddesses and assorted deities ruling the universe as Paul argued. Their sexual proclivities and polytheism were reminiscent of the Canaanites.

The Egyptians purportedly worshiped many gods usually through Pharaoh as their mediator but Egyptian theology was much more complex than that. Theological changes were common depending upon leadership but monotheism ruled, while many subordinate entities were venerated. This was the pattern except for when Pharaoh Akhenaten took the throne as he totally changed the religious system of Egypt by only worshipping one god and eliminating veneration of any other entity, which also included priesthood changes. He ruled years prior to Moses.[206]

---

[206] "A History of Israel - John Bright - Google Books." 1 Jan. 2000, https://books.google.com/books/about/A_History_of_Israel.html?id=0VG67yLs-LAC.

Scholars are deeply divided on dating the exodus from Egypt but we can be sure that the pharaoh "who did not know Moses" was not Akhenaten or even his son King Tutankamen (King Tut). Chancellor Williams, Cheikh Diop and others truly opened our understanding of the religion and skin color of Africa transforming the world's concept of African peoples. Challenges to their scholarship are easily debunked by modern genetics which support Williams' and Diop's description of migrations and blending of people groups for the time period studied.[207] Race and religion issues dominate factors that affect socioeconomic status and the Egyptian race and religion controversy is the major starting point. The patterns begin here and continue until this day.

As in today the method of assimilation of light/dark skinned peoples along with religious doctrine become flashpoints. A Harvard University researcher recently stated: "For instance, alt-right proponents have stated,

---

[207] "Ancient Egyptian mummy genomes suggest an increase of ... - Nature." 30 May. 2017, https://www.nature.com/articles/ncomms15694.

correctly, that many people with European and Asian descent have inherited 1-4% of their DNA from Neanderthal ancestors. They are similarly correct that Neanderthals had larger skulls than humans. Based on these facts, some within the alt-right community have claimed that Europeans and Asians have superior intelligence because they have inherited larger brains from their Neanderthal ancestors."[208] The problem is that researchers have found Neanderthal ancestry in African populations also.[209] Others claim that race isn't a social construct based upon factors such as sickle cell rates and lactose intolerance which occur more frequently in people of African descent.[210] A survey of

---

[208] "How Science and Genetics are Reshaping the Race Debate of the ...." 17 Apr. 2017, http://sitn.hms.harvard.edu/flash/2017/science-genetics-reshaping-race-debate-21st-century/.

[209] "New study identifies Neanderthal ancestry in African ...."https://www.princeton.edu/news/2020/01/30/new-study-identifies-neanderthal-ancestry-african-populations-and-describes-its.

[210] "Why White Supremacists Are Chugging Milk (and Why Geneticists Are ...." 17 Oct. 2018, https://www.nytimes.com/2018/10/17/us/white-supremacists-science-dna.html.

intelligence experts found that 94% believe that the higher IQ of whites was due to genetic factors.[211] Race science is embedding even more deeply into scholarly journals and universities with this craziness.[212] An excellent anthropologist, Catherine Townsend quotes Adam Rutherford's book "How to Argue with a Racists" on Twitter: "Modern genetics clearly shows that the way we colloquially define race does not align with the biology that underpins human variation. Instead, race is a cultural taxonomy – a social construct. This doesn't mean it's invalid or unimportant, nor does it mean race does not exist."[213] Facts are not strong enough to overtake evil because the devil is a liar. Racism is evil.

[211] "Survey of expert opinion on intelligence - ScienceDirect.com." https://www.sciencedirect.com/science/article/pii/S0160289619301886.

[212] "Whitewashing Scientific Racism: Revisiting the Equalitarian ...." 31 Jan. 2020, https://altrightorigins.com/2020/01/31/whitewashing-scientific-racism/.

[213] "Twitter." https://twitter.com/CathrynTownsend/status/1221814289704587266

Viewing the religion of the Pharaohs that the Copts of Egypt practiced gives us a beautiful perspective of mankind's struggles today. Hoards of African Americans are flocking to Egyptian based religions and fleeing Christianity because of Christianity's association with the slave trade and genocide. They are ignoring the deep rooted Christianity of Egypt, Ethiopia and Nubia. 20 years after Constantine issued the Edict of Milan decriminalizing Christianity and 47 years before Theodosius I made Christianity the state religion of the Roman Empire, King Ezana, ruler of the kingdom of Aksum, made Christinity the state religion of Ethiopia. Christianity entered Nubia in the 5th century through missionaries from Egypt. Islam intitially militarily forced its way into Africa with strong resistance from Christian African nations but it was Nubia who did not allow itself to be conquered, maintaining its Christian identity until the sixteenth century when migrations of Islamic ethnic groups caused it to die out. Sub-Saharan Africa had stable, strong Christian nations from the early church until today.[214] The story has to be told because ancient Egypt is seen as a bastion of intellect and black strength and therefore many are believing the worship of the gods of Egypt would be a return to Africa's former glory six thousand years ago. YouTube has become a teaching foundation for new theologies and ideologies to fit almost any desire. Physicians and pastors who ignore the forces shifting the minds of members and patients are destined to become irrelevant in shaping the motivations and desires of their patients and members.

True monotheistic worship changes a society. JD Unwin studied 86 civilizations and found that monogamous cultures developed while sexually loose cultures dissolved. The strong family unit is a hallmark of true monotheistic worship. The relationship between worship and homeostasis should be able to be measured. Worship of the one true God promises perfect peace, joy, health and strength leading to better

---

[214] "Early African Christianity: Nubia — Jude 3 Project." 29 Sep. 2016, https://jude3project.org/blog/2016/earlychristianitynubia.

communities and a better life. Homeostasis means a life in balance. If we review history, we should see a relationship between the level of homeostasis within people, their community, their environment and their neighbors. Christianity recognizes this in the bible in Romans 1:20: "For since the creation of the world His invisible *attributes* are clearly seen, being understood by the things that are made, *even* His eternal power and Godhead, so that they are without excuse." Also Romans 2:14: "For when the Gentiles, which have not the law, do by nature the things contained in the law, these, having not the law, are a law unto themselves." We should be able to look at any society and measure their life wellbeing by their true worship regardless of the professed beliefs. As we have seen, so called Christian communities have lived as devil worshippers while carrying the cross of Christ. For those, Christ distinctly stated in Matthew 7:21-23 "Not everyone who says to Me, 'Lord, Lord,' shall enter the kingdom of heaven, but he who does the will of My Father in heaven. Many will say to Me in that day, 'Lord, Lord, have we not prophesied in Your name, cast out demons

in Your name, and done many wonders in Your name?'
And then I will declare to them, 'I never knew you;
depart from Me, you who practice lawlessness!'".
Homeostasis then does not relate directly to professed
religious beliefs but to a deeper worship of God. As
Fuller described: "Monotheism is therefore not only a
powerful constraint on the models we build, it is also a
first step toward opening the quest for truth to
outsiders and amateurs, who may see things differently
than the establishment. Buried within the model of
monotheism lies the democratic ideal of no favored
status." [215] He also stated: "Monotheism is the
theological counterpart of the scientist's belief in the
ultimate reconcilability of apparently contradictory
observations into one consistent framework."
The religion of the pharaohs of Egypt then is described
as a purely polythiestic society but so is Christianity in
the worship of three Gods. To the casual observer, the
concept of one God in three persons is pure polytheism.

---

[215] "Why One God Is Better Than Ten | Psychology Today." 1 Jul.
2012,
https://www.psychologytoday.com/us/blog/somebodies-and-nobodi
es/201207/why-one-god-is-better-ten.

Add the pentacostal doctrine that sees the power of the apostles as being still available today, then to that observer, trouble begins. Paul talked about it in the early church's meeting where members spoke in tongues without an interpreter. He said please continue to speak in tongues but not around people who did not believe as they would see them as insane.

Believers are to believe in the power of the anointing, the work of angels, the influence of demon spirits, the resurrection of the dead and handkerchiefs that had healing power. To the casual observer all of those would be gods. Paul again encountered Greeks who saw his anointing and thought he was a god and worshiped him. Worship of one God should include the view of the Godhead which is God almighty, God who forgives and God present at all times within the lives of believers. There should be a heart change leading to a behavior change: homeostasis. Telomere length[216] and DNA methylation[217] (with subsequent changes in belly fat)

[216] "Racial discrimination and telomere shortening among African ...." 13 Jan. 2020, https://psycnet.apa.org/doiLanding?doi=10.1037%2Fhea0000832.

[217] "DNA methylation-based estimator of telomere ... - NCBI - NIH." 18 Aug. 2019, https://www.ncbi.nlm.nih.gov/pubmed/31422385.

should be able to reflect society's life peace. Those societies should have less war. Douglas Fry pointed out in his book Beyond War: The Human Potential for Peace, that "for perhaps ninety-nine percent of our history, for well over a million years, humans lived in nomadic hunter-and-gatherer groups, egalitarian bands where generosity was highly valued and warfare was a rarity." [218] The issue is determining the hearts of the people to see if they are monothiestic or polythiestic in ancient times. Chancellor Williams described Egypt and sub-Saharan Africa as monothiestic. W. M. Flinders Petrie in his book, the Religion of Ancient Egypt also described many Egyptian dynasties as being monotheistic but changed depending upon the Pharaoh. The numerous god deities many times were subordinate to an all powerful god, or the Pharaoh would be the conduit by which people would hear from god. The Egyptian Book of the Dead, which is often cited, isn't able to accurately communicate the true

---

[218] "Beyond war: The human potential for peace. - APA PsycNET." http://psycnet.apa.org/record/2007-05299-000.

beliefs of the people.[219] History, science and religion aren't capable enough to fully describe spiritual conditions but the insight is amazing. The ancient Egyptians believed in the hearts being weighed to determine their fate in the afterlife. This would entail forgiveness and righteous living. The heart, not the brain, was the source of wisdom and upon death, the heart was weighed. "In the weighing of the heart rite, the heart of the deceased was weighed on a scale against the feather of the goddess Maat, who personifies order, truth, and what is right."[220]

The ancient Egyptians struggled with race. The natural desire of people to maintain their family culture is genetically encoded. Like likes like, where differences create fear.[221] The greater the difference in skin tones, the greater the fear therefore between light skinned and

[219] "The Religion of Ancient Egypt by W. M. Flinders Petrie." 31 May. 2009, https://www.gutenberg.org/ebooks/29010.
[220] "The book of death: weighing your heart - NCBI." https://www.ncbi.nlm.nih.gov/pmc/articles/PMC3960665/.
[221] "When Social Fear Disappears, So Does Racism | Science | AAAS." 12 Apr. 2010, https://www.sciencemag.org/news/2010/04/when-social-fear-disappears-so-does-racism.

dark skinned people the difference is huge. Since dark skinned people can easily assimilate because of the huge variations in acceptable skin tones, they have a huge advantage to be able to mix with lighter skinned people without fear. Africa has more genetic diversity than anywhere else in the world and we were diverse in skin color before leaving Africa.[222] Whereas so called "white" people can lose their identity upon mixing with a dark skinned person forever. It is easy to see the immense fear. Even though true genetic differences are incongruent with skin color and other exterior features, the fear is understandable but still wrong. Ancient Egypt followed this pattern. As northwest semetic people flowed in from areas of less resources to the fertile crescent which had plentiful resources, particularly advanced Egypt, they found welcoming so called "black" people along the overflowing Nile river. The Nile provided rich soil and stable living.[223] A waist

---

[222] "Twitter."
https://twitter.com/CathrynTownsend/status/122379208439991910
5.
[223] "War Is Not Part of Human Nature - Scientific American."
1 Sep. 2018,

to hip ratio of near 0.7 is most attractive and African women have a higher propensity of having larger hips therefore generally would be more attractive at the same waist measurement.[224] [225] Combining these factors created the conditions where the light skinned male invader would be aroused by and have sex with the black woman but not accept their child since lighter skin was and still is seen as reflecting more intelligence, value, culture, etc... Their children would still have better treatment than the other darker skinned family though. The black man would be seen as less powerful [226] creating divisions between black men and black women. "For in Egypt, as elsewhere, it was a one-way sexual process." Chancellor Williams explained: "the 'master race' always kept its own women 'sacred' and

https://www.scientificamerican.com/article/war-is-not-part-of-human-nature/.

[224] "The Relationship Between Waist-Hip Ratio and Fertility | Psychology ...." 19 Jun. 2017, https://www.psychologytoday.com/us/blog/beastly-behavior/201706/the-relationship-between-waist-hip-ratio-and-fertility.

[225] "Steatopygia - Human Phenotypes." http://humanphenotypes.net/metrics/steatopygia.html.

[226] "Benevolent Sexism and Mate Preferences: Why Do ... - SAGE Journals." https://journals.sagepub.com/doi/abs/10.1177/0146167218781000.

secluded behind the walls of their homes. They were not allowed to go outside except under guard. African women had no such restrictions or protection."[227] This pattern can be seen over and over until this day. This formula of resource attraction, sex attraction, and skin color fragility has been a force transcending religions, continents, ethnicities, education and time. Kudos to the many who have ignored, resisted or exposed the internal and external temptations to flow along this vile river.

This huge race controversy of Egypt is so critical. Their technological advances, being able to construct pyramids using the Pythagorean theorem, algebra and trigonometry along with mummification, complex societies and more, makes the ancient Egyptians a coveted team to be on. What's comical is that the standard for being black in my neighborhood is one drop. I have many friends that look Caucasian but you'll never see their white family members at a reunion,

---

[227] "Destruction of Black Civilization: Great Issues of a Race from ...." https://www.amazon.com/Destruction-Black-Civilization-Issues-D/dp/0883780305.

neither would you see them at mine, but everyone in Egypt was black, almost all of the bible is black including Jesus using 7th ward New Orleans' rules. All Jews are black. Afro-Asian is black just as Afro-American is black. Genetically, the whole world is black.[228] Using the one drop rule, Hitler was black and he killed 6 million Jews because of the black in them with their origin being Afro-Asian.[229] The advances of Egypt came up from Nubia/Ethiopia, not down. Egypt was northern Ethiopia before it became two-lands. The invaders came down and pushed everyone further down. Chicago sang Colour My World...

As we travel through Egyptian history we see it is African history where the formula of resource attraction, sex attraction and skin color fagility pushed darker skinned people further south. The desire for

[228] "How to Argue with a Racist by Adam Rutherford review – how ...." 30 Jan. 2020, https://www.theguardian.com/books/2020/jan/30/how-to-argue-with-a-racist-adam-rutherford-review.
[229] "All Africans under the Skin | National Geographic Society." https://www.nationalgeographic.org/activity/all-africans-under-the-skin/.

survival from cold climates and low resources stimulated the fight or flight sympathetic nervous system responses in addition to the pleasurable excitement of great weather and the gorgeous Beyonce type waist to hip ratios that would send dopamine levels sky high. The further south they traveled, the more gold was found and traded bringing financial prosperity.[230] Dopamine is the main pleasure neurotransmitter which is activated in cocaine addiction. Sex, comfort and money are powerful stimulators that only true monotheism can turn off.

Kevin MacLeod produced an excellent study that described the average temperature of Egypt and Mesopotamia as being the perfect locations for comfort therefore geography becomes another confounder to explain the early attraction and advancement of those civilizations.[231] In addition to waist to hip ratios which

---

[230] "Gold The True Motor Of West African History: An Overview Of ...."
http://rozenbergquarterly.com/gold-the-true-motor-of-west-african-history-an-overview-of-the-importance-of-gold-in-west-africa-and-its-relations-with-the-wider-world-2/.
[231] "https://www.youtube.com/watch?v=oG19fCFSa ... - Facebook."
https://www.facebook.com/permalink.php?id=332927164023500&story_fbid=368592147123668.

can be adjusted by diet, female lumbar curvature has consistently registered as an indicator of male sexual attraction with a 45 degree angle being the most attractive. Research validates an arched back as being common in women of African descent.[232] [233] In today's culture, high heels simulate an arched back, also twerking type dances accentuate the area therefore the visual stimulation resulting in increased attraction is strong and should be expected since it is hormonally mediated.[234]

Monotheism's effects on the mind and heart leads people to naturally treat people the same way they would want to be treated because from the monotheistic perspective all people are created in the

[232] "Racial differences in sacral structure important in ... - NCBI."
https://www.ncbi.nlm.nih.gov/pubmed/453583.
[233] "Men's Preference for Certain Body Types Has Evolutionary ...."
19 Mar. 2015,
https://news.utexas.edu/2015/03/19/mens-preference-for-certain-body-types-has-evolutionary-roots/.
[234] "Arching the Back (Lumbar Curvature) as a Female Sexual ...."
25 Oct. 2017,
https://link.springer.com/article/10.1007/s40806-017-0123-7.

image of one God.[235] The heart change would bring peace to halt anyone from abusing women because they would be children of the same father God. It would halt the skin color fragility because all people would be equal regardless of color. It would halt the forced taking of resources because no one would want their resources taken from them. Monotheism connects us together as one under one Father. Polytheism is relative. Monotheism is natural and connects us as one. Polytheism divides us into groups based upon separate gods, freeing the passions and desires to abuse or neglect others based upon the needs of their self and/or their god. Strict, legalistic discipline can order society to appear kind and gentle but the true reality of altruism is reflected in the heart and actions, with the truth eventually being observed. Monotheistic religions can actually be polytheistic if they allow worship of their law and not the Spirit (God). They can also separate the one God into distinct gods in an unbalanced way. Belief

---

[235] "Why One God Is Better Than Ten | Psychology Today." 1 Jul. 2012, https://www.psychologytoday.com/us/blog/somebodies-and-nobodies/201207/why-one-god-is-better-ten.

in the trinity should still be a belief in one God but
tribalism has led to the utter separation and creation of
deep divisions while claiming to worship one God.
Polytheistic religions could very well be monotheistic
depending upon the actual power of the other gods. As
in Egypt, many periods and people were actually
monotheistic with other so called "gods" deriving all
power from one all powerful God. This varied as
invaders brought in their gods and intertwined their
theologies with that of Egypt. The power flow is always
the only dividing line. Egypt's challenges reflect the
triad of sexual attraction to black women's shape,
resource lust, and skin color fragility, unchecked by love
and altruism. Love and its subsequent altruism results
from true monotheism.

Their methods of economic domination haven't
changed for thousands of years. Prior to the 1st dynasty,
Egypt was divided into two lands because of Asian
migrations/invasions. It was originally Northern
Ethiopia (Egypt) and Southern Ethiopia (Sudan). The
great achievements came from Meroe and Napata in the

south and flowed up to create this wondrous civilization further up the Nile river. The Asians flowed in as traders. The trading posts became fortifications geographically located near the waterways allowing them easy access to Europe and Asia. They eventually took control over one-fourth of the land until in 3100, the Ehiopian leader Menes reunited the "Two Lands" and started the dynastic system which lasted until 2181 with the sixth dynasty which was also the end of the Old Kingdom. This method began with Asian invaders and continued with European invaders for over 5000 years until the pan African liberation movements in Africa and the Caribbean expelled the colonialist but still leaving the United States in a period of mass incarceration. Mass incarceration is defined as the systematic imprisonment of masses of black people by using "stop and frisk", profiling, enhanced arrests, enhanhanced convictions and longer prison sentences for the same crimes that other races commit while systematically sustaining an economic and cultural environment that nourishes that incarceration system. This is mass incarceration.

Yes, great black civilizations were created beginning prior to the Old Kingdom in Egypt which saw the greatest achievements still marveled at until this day with the pyramids still standing. Biology and economics present a clear picture of the history of black people. All aspects of domination continue though with gentrification, with raised housing prices and with other people groups taking the best lands while still being voted in political offices by "black" people. Economically powerful "black" men consistently marry down to lower economic class "white" women transferring wealth out of the community. Black women are sought after for some jobs and are the most educated while the poorer black men lag behind through more mass incarceration. The lighter the woman's skin, the more valuable she is. Darker skinned women are being shunned as racism is as bad within the black community as outside. The demoralized black man self destructs while continually degrading the black woman, all being cut off from trade routes, valuable land, access to capital and education: from pyramids to projects. The slavery, segregation, mass incarceration triad shouldn't be underestimated as illicit drugs becomes a major economic driver within a gentrified community, setting the stage for police sweeps and drug territory killings that charachterize much of the community.[236] The destruction of black male masculinity becomes the driver of an anti-marriage, self hate, family and business destroying culture. The so called black collegiate intelligentsia has adopted millennial male feminization as being in vogue and attractive, fitting into the dehumanized, racist destruction of the black family. God never designed the anus to be sexually penetrated whereas the resulting blood and feces illustrate the destruction of honor and homeostasis.[237] [238] [239] [240] The power of sex is

---

[236] "Christopher Sylvain (@ChrisSylvain) | Twitter."https://twitter.com/ChrisSylvain/status/1192060919033028609?s=20

[237] "Anal Intercourse and Fecal Incontinence: Evidence ... - NCBI." 12 Jan. 2016, https://www.ncbi.nlm.nih.gov/pmc/articles/PMC5231615/.

[238] "Is anal sex safe? 6 potential risks to avoid - Medical News Today." 6 Mar. 2019, https://www.medicalnewstoday.com/articles/324637.php.

[239] "Anal sex practices in heterosexual and male homosexual - NCBI." https://www.ncbi.nlm.nih.gov/pubmed/22951046.

proportional to its polarity and commitment, defined by sexual homeostasis.

Africa was taken over by pushing the people further inward creating trauma and turmoil with Asian rulers taking the throne as Pharaoh and integrating their gods. The history has been deliberately hidden to obliterate the black achievements but the results have been highlighted. Just as weak African kings were unable to band together therefore existed as small independent kingdoms - the black church today is unable to see the reality of powers against its people and the necessity of joining together.

The pressure on whites to accept skin color fragility is huge. A person would have to fight generations of scientific attacks led by nobel prize winning scientists who are bragging about the inferiority of black people in prestigious scientific journals. They would have to fight many of their religious leaders who also condone overt racism. The costs are huge for any whites who

---

[240] "Heterosexual anal intercourse: a neglected risk ... - NCBI - NIH." 24 Dec. 2012, https://www.ncbi.nlm.nih.gov/pubmed/23279040.

attempt to bridge the gap. The world should salute those brave souls but understand the pressures of being an abolitionist. The biological drive to desire the shape of black women has lasted and is more powerful than the economic drivers creating divisions of major proportions. The fair skinned children are tempted to band together, marry together, demoralizing their mothers and darker skinned family as the fathers rarely acknowledge their actions. During slavery, light skinned women were called "Fancy Girls" being sold for higher prices than the most powerful black male buck. The dehumanization and castration of black male masculinity is a direct consequence of watching his wives, sisters and mothers being prostituted. The lighter skinned blacks who resist the temptation should be more celebrated. Even dark skinned blacks fall into the same trap and deny their African heritage while accentuating the smallest bit of European features.

Monotheism existed long before Abraham and Moses as people always had access to God. It alone provides the foundation to unite all people groups harmoniously.

Polytheism by definition accepts a divided god therefore a divided people. God chose an Afro-Asian people to carry His law pulling Abraham out of Mesopotamia. By the time Joseph was brought to Egypt, the Asian Hyksos had taken over the throne starting the 2nd intermediate period. Just as Menes (a black man) united the two lands to begin the Old Kingdom 700 years earlier, Ahmose (a black man) reunited the two lands of Upper and Lower Egypt but enslaved the Hebrews and expelled the Hyksos. Just as the Asians before them, the Hyksos came to Egypt because of better resources. They began trading and occupying good land. They married up into royalty. Many believed that the Hyksos took the power without using their considerable military resources but by using the Hyksos women, just as some rich black football and basketball players regularly seek non-black women.[241] After taking power the Hyksos used the same system of white leaders using black women as property,

---

[241] "Foreigners peacefully conquered ancient Egypt through ...." 2 Apr. 2019, https://www.sciencenews.org/article/mysterious-hyksos-dynasty-conquered-ancient-egypt-marriage.

furthering the light skin - dark skin divisions. This system debases black women since again, lighter skinned children of their white fathers were given special privileges while debasing and emasculating black men as they were forced to observe their women being prostituted. The Hyksos brought the worship of Baal into the pantheon which was a wicked, debased polytheism. Baal worshippers engaged in rituals of homosexual and heterosexual sex, burned children in fire as sacrifices and worshipped golden and other graven images. The monothiestic Hebrews, listed as Apiru in Egyptian literature, may have been victims of mistaken identity. They were not polytheistic Hyksos, but monotheistic.

The biblical tradition in light of the archeological evidence continually has challenges but those challenges are totally irrelevant. Science and theology are two totally different disciplines. We will have many questions when we get to heaven. Science should always end with a question. It is not designed to produce "beliefs" but information. The confounding variables and infinite possibilities along with no controlled studies leaves archeology in a weak position to disturb the biblical text. The practical reality though is that archeology adds depth and beautiful background to the text. It's the same with evolution and Darwinian theory. The mathematical challenges, challenges in molecular biology, newly discovered horizontal gene transfer and more are upsetting the Darwinian apple cart. Challenges are not close to being accepted as I was destroyed on Twitter[242] for even presenting David Gelernter, an esteemed scientist's case questioning Darwin. I asked three well respected geneticists their views of Gelernter's essay and all three (Bierny, Mitchell and Turkheimer) along with a caravan of others denounced it but their responses were within the context of science, meaning confident but not ideological. The bible is of course ideological and reaches past anything science could imagine. We're discussing when Moses parted the Red Sea! The Hebrews walked across on dry land. The bible can't be

[242] "Twitter."
https://twitter.com/ChrisSylvain/status/1177128613201752065.

proven wrong and science shouldn't try because it is of a different realm. Let's keep it separate. Science should know its limits. It can't figure out consciousness yet, or 1 million starling birds flying in unison, or the impossibility of the universe even existing. Let it figure out how and why processed foods are toxic. Faith by definition defies science therefore life defies science. Science is wonderful and mandatory but it is limited in answering life's big questions: who are we and why are we here. Science doesn't do well at looking holistically at life in context. It's driven by reductionism but God can't be reduced. It has a need to reduce every question to its smallest part but it keeps getting confused. Biology is not applied chemistry. In the body it keeps finding new guys that make things happen. A guy affects this old guy who finds a new guy and makes the cell move in a new way. In chemistry, then physics it keeps finding smaller guys smaller than the smallest guy like chemical molecules, then atoms, then smaller particles, then strings. They want to build a gadget bigger than the Large Hadron Collider to find smaller guys trying to figure out the big guys. Science's job is to find an answer. If it doesn't find an answer scientists get embarrassed and rarely will publish their work (null results).[243] Evolution has mathematical issues but to imagine the possibility of the existence of other forces goes against science, so scientists create a tight culture of scientism, waiting on more studies but still accepting their "theory". Astrophysics has mathematical issues where the universe appears to be fine tuned by another force or else it would blow up. Instead of accepting a creator, science comes up with more universes and they are serious. They say: well since our numbers don't work here there must be more universes with more numbers we hadn't figured out yet. This is real comic book stuff from legitimate people. Whenever you stretch science whether in the body to particles of matter to the universe itself, science answers: I don't know. The Bible does know though. We can believe the Bible and still study science for color and background. It's fun, beautiful and biblical.

[243] "Scientists offered €1,000 to publish null results | Times Higher ...." 11 Feb. 2020, https://www.timeshighereducation.com/news/scientists-offered-eu1000-publish-null-results. Accessed 12 Feb. 2020.

So the biblical text appears to correspond to Ramses II
as Pharaoh during the exodus to Canaan. The Dead Sea
Scrolls verifies the accuracy of the biblical texts along
with possibly the Ebla Texts and Nuzi documents as if it
needs it. Remember the biblical text is at least 1200
years younger than older Egypian and Mesopotamian
documents.

Race drove black Africa further south over centuries
with black Africa responding powerfully but the
eventual push from Asians mixed and dominated
almost at will, leaving black Africa weakened. More
study is needed but the theological argument must be
made: was the dilution of monotheism in black Egypt
the deeper cause of its decimation? Is it much easier for
monotheism to exist with other subservient small gods
and powerful ancestors than to improperly worship a
triune God? Can a so called polytheistic religion
actually be monotheistic while a monotheistic religion
can actually be practiced as polytheism? More later but
the Hebrews were the people given the perfect

monotheistic text, prophets along with miracles, cloud by day and fire by night but still couldn't get it right. Dopamine driven addictions mixed with polytheistic religious worship tempted these people beyond their ability to contain. The choir hit the red light district. Through great leadership Israel thrived with God's power on display overtaking the Cannanites, Amorites, Arameans, the European Philistines[244] [245] and others but eventually were destroyed leaving only a remnant. God does not show favoritism to any race because race is only a social construct. The Hebrews left Egypt with a "mixed" multitude of other ethnic groups. They were Afro-Asian before going into Egypt but definitely mixed while there and by including the mixed multitude when leaving Egypt, the assimilation continued strongly. Mixture is why Hitler created the holocaust, killing 6 million Jews. On August 11, 2017 in Charlottesville,Va.

---

[244] "Ancient DNA reveals the Biblical-era Philistines originated in ...." 3 Jul. 2019,
https://www.sciencenews.org/article/ancient-dna-origins-philistines-bible-europe-israel.
[245] "Vorfahren der biblischen Philister kamen aus Europa | Max ...." 3 Jul. 2019,
https://www.shh.mpg.de/1359905/ashkelon-philistines-feldman.

Donald Trump's (with 81% white evangelical support[246]) "very fine people" people marched to the chant: "Jews will not replace us".[247]

The relationship between Egypt and Israel was complex. The Bible recounts in 2 Chronicles an invasion from Pharaoh Shishak (Shashonq)[248] along with Ethiopians and Libyans during Rehoboam's reign in Judah because of disobedience to the Lord. Later the Prophet Isaiah warned against trusting Egypt (the powerful Ethiopian 25th dynasty) to help the smaller southern kingdom, Judah fight against the Assyrians. By then the northern kingdom of Israel had already fallen to the Assyrians. Amos preached fiercely against the economic injustices of Israel while Hosea preached

---

[246] "Influential evangelical leader on why Trump will ... - Fox News." 16 Jan. 2020, https://www.foxnews.com/faith-values/trump-prayer-god-2020-election-schools.

[247] "Adam Serwer: White Nationalism's Deep ... - The Atlantic." https://www.theatlantic.com/magazine/archive/2019/04/adam-serwer-madison-grant-white-nationalism/583258/.

[248] "Did Pharaoh Sheshonq Attack Jerusalem? - Biblical ...." 27 Jul. 2012, https://www.biblicalarchaeology.org/daily/biblical-topics/hebrew-bible/did-pharaoh-sheshonq-attack-jerusalem/.

against their drunkenness and sexuality which was all the result of their syncretism. Their strength was monotheism and without it they were impotent. Micah preached powerfully to Judah to worship only one God sincerely and to stop being hypocrites. Their love of money screamed hypocrisy while the prophet Micah responded like a trumpet declaring that they should shut their church (temple) doors because their songs and sacrifices would not be accepted. Assyria, Babylon, Persia, Greece, and Rome conquered Egypt and Israel bringing us back to the time of Christ. Assyria's invasion of Egypt created the 26th dynasty and ended the Egyptian rule. From the beginning, the northern invasions pushed darker skinned people further south, destabilizing sub-Saharan Africa.

Sub-Saharan Africa

But just as much of Egypt was monotheistic, so was sub-Saharan Africa. Defining monotheism is the key. Veneration in and of itself does not constitute polytheism. African traditional religion venerated ancestors and various deities but all being subservient to one all powerful and knowing God. Over the thousands of years various belief systems took place among many groups. From the perspective of traditional African religion, the classifications appear irrelevant as spirituality penetrated every aspect of life, all emanating from an all powerful supreme being. The discussion is spiritual and beyond mental comprehension. The closest concept would be the trinity which is unexplainable in human terms. Dr. John Mbiti is recognized as the premiere scholar on African traditional religion and he describes the God of Abraham as the God of African people.[249] The reflection

---

[249] "The Encounter of Christian Faith and African Religion ...." https://www.religion-online.org/article/the-encounter-of-christian-fait h-and-african-religion/.

is the speed by which Christianity was peacefully adopted throughout Africa. Again, Romans 1:20 becomes our guidepost that by seeing the creation we should see the Godhead at any time and anywhere in the world. The manifestation would be the fruit of the spirit of those people: love, joy, peace, kindness, gentleness, self control which just like the Egyptian heart needing to be lighter than a feather, becoming recognized as an ancestor in African traditional religion required living a righteous life.

The life structure opened the door for holistic mentorship and training. Family background did not alone place people in positions of leadership. They had to be qualified. Training began with children, then ages 13-18, 19-28, 29-40, then 40 and over. Each grade class had expectations and training, creating an ecosystem for them to develop. Grades were divided also by male and female. The 19-28 grade also composed the fighting forces which included a women's battalion. Being over 40 allowed someone to be eligible to be a part of the esteemed council of elders. This was a supreme honor and privilege. Behavioral expectations were built into each age grade creating an enduring culture of respect and morality. The chief was the mouthpiece of the people only, as the people (together) had all the power, but the people humbly recognized a supreme God as having all power.

This is the environment that the immoral enslavers and missionaries entered into. They were bringing a polythiestic so called Christian gospel to a people who knew God for themselves. Their refusal to acknowledge the power of the Holy Spirit created an unbalanced view of God relegating the Holy Spirit as a separate weak being, who was not empowering, filling, nor anointing. They were as legalistic as the pharisees. To control the membership, churches would not teach about the power of the Holy Spirit. They definitely couldn't teach the slaves about His power.

Ewan Birney tweeted: "the differences we see here in these very broad self identified ethnic groups are predominantly cultural and societal, e.g. socioeconomic status (wealth)." He along with Rutherford, Raff and Scally wrote a powerful piece debunking the theory of race as a biological concept.[250] Sex differences are biologically distinct with only 1 in 5000 people being intersex.[251] Race differences are not. History moves on skin color but biology doesn't. Theology shouldn't, but when out of balance, it will. Collective doctrine doesn't necessarily affect individual worship. The Christians who enslaved Africans were doctrinally corrupt but that same doctrine could have assisted the salvation of slaves or others. We can accept Christ without reading the Bible as the thief on the cross did, so the enslavers doctrine hindered but didn't eliminate God. This is important because even today with various denominations and doctrines everywhere, we must be aware that just because a person belongs to a certain denomination, that doesn't in and of itself validate their personal beliefs. Anyone can be saved regardless of denomination or religion. It's by faith in God with that

[250] "Race, genetics and pseudoscience: an explainer - Ewan's Blog." 24 Oct. 2019, http://ewanbirney.com/2019/10/race-genetics-and-pseudoscience-an-explainer.html.
[251] "Large-scale GWAS reveals insights into the genetic ... - Science." 30 Aug. 2019, https://science.sciencemag.org/content/365/6456/eaat7693.

faith being represented by works. Presentation of the true gospel will lead them to Christ as He is God as Son. The denominational beliefs though are forever tainted by the horrors of slavery particularly the treatment of women.

The Church in Context

It is in this context that modern Christianity must be viewed and subsequently the role of the pastor. The current denominations are all shaped by slavery. Healthcare is shaped by race through slavery.[252]

So now we can return to events in the church after having looked at the Christian church in its historical context which included Africa. There must be more scholarship to provide a non-racist church history that includes Africa because the same forces that drive people's behaviors also drive researchers. Prior to the Reformation one of the largest splits came from the oriental churches including the Christian churches of Africa moving away from the Roman Catholic and Orthodox churches because of differences in the view of Jesus. In 451 at the Council of Chalcedon, the challenge arose when the oriental churches refused to accept a

---

[252] "the geography of child opportunity: why ... - Diversitydatakids.org."
http://new.diversitydatakids.org/sites/default/files/2020-01/ddk_the-geography-of-child-opportunity_2020.pdf.

theology that separated the divine and human natures of Christ. They use the term miaphysitism, meaning the human and divine nature of Christ is one, as opposed to dyophysitism which is the belief in two natures of Christ in one person. The split was north/south generally along cultural and racial lines. The next major split was an east/west split in 1054 where the Orthodox Church split from the Roman Catholic Church over papal supremacy whereas originally the patriarch of Alexandria in Egypt, along with the popes of the Orthodox church and others were all equal, but the Bishop of Rome changed and claimed authority over the Orthodox and other patriarchs. This was in addition to issues of celibacy and whether the Holy Spirit proceeded from the Son and the Father or only from the Father. Also a major dispute was the Roman Catholic decision to object to marriages to sixth cousins or closer. To this day behaviors in communities around the world where the Roman Catholic Church penetrated, result in less intensive kinship, greater individualism, less conformity, and more trust toward strangers.[253] Other research shows that those same countries are much more accepting of homosexuality, all because of forcing people to marry outside of their group therefore destalilizing the family unit.[254] All other Christian countries exhibited close kinship and family trust through a church doctrine of only claiming incest if marrying less than the third cousins, allowing true family stabilization and less promotion of homosexuality. These issues and more caused the east/west split which lasts until this day. The gargantuan change in society's values because of this doctrinal decision could not be overstated as it illustrates the power of church doctrine in changing the world.

This brings us back to the Protestant Reformation which we discussed already but moving forward, a group of the radical reformers called Anabaptist created one of the largest shifts in how the church operated in

---

[253] "The Church, intensive kinship, and global ... - Science." 8 Nov. 2019, https://science.sciencemag.org/content/366/6466/eaau5141.
[254] "The Global Divide on Homosexuality | Pew ...." 4 Jun. 2013, https://www.pewresearch.org/global/2013/06/04/the-global-divide-on-homosexuality/.

society since Constantine. They pushed sanctification more than the magisterial reformers: Ulrich Zwingli and John Calvin who pushed a spiritual life (sanctification) more than Martin Luther. The Anabaptists (rebaptizers) began by resisting participation in the military but some eventually became violent themselves. Catholics and Protestants alike were intent on wiping out Anabaptists. They persecuted anyone who accepted or especially preached the Anabaptist message seeing this so-called heresy as a spiritual disease that threatened the souls of men and women as well as the stability of society. As such, Anabaptists were tortured, mocked, starved, imprisoned, beheaded, burned and drowned. And many Anabaptists expected nothing less than to suffer for their faith.[255]

The Church of England followed the worship and governance of the Catholic Church but was influenced by John Calvin and Martin Luther. Angelican and

---

[255] "Do Baptists spring from Anabaptist seed? - Baptist Press." 3 Jul. 2017, http://www.bpnews.net/49158/do-baptists-spring-from-anabaptist-seed.

Episcopal churches flow from their tradition. Founding the Methodist movement, John Wesley broke from the Church of England to pursue spiritualist methods in every aspect of inner and outer life through the Holy Spirit. Also from the Church of England, George Fox and notably his follower William Penn, who founded Pennsylvania, insisted that one only needed the Holy Spirit and not even the Bible was necessary. These were called Quakers. The Baptist Church's origins are of much debate with some insisting on Anabaptists origins and others, Church of England origins by John Smyth. Others follow a line stemming from the time of Christ. So called Christian polytheism that doesn't open the door to spiritual lifestyles, music, art and dance but locks them into a church box is fertile ground for racism. Race and sex are the big two passions that fight against our spirit. Suppressing the Holy Spirit leads to racism. Suppressing the power of the resurrection leads to racism. Doctrine affects faith which affects behavior. Church doctrine doesn't determine a person's faith alone but it can have a powerful effect as it is the system

by which people are fed the word. Doctrine forms
beliefs which drive culture.

The Pentecostal movement was catalyzed by a
Wesleyan Holiness African American preacher, William
Seymour on Azusa Street in Los Angeles in 1906. It was
the Yale University historian Sidney Ahlstrom who said
Seymour personified a black piety "which exerted its
greatest direct influence on American religious
history"—placing Seymour's impact ahead of figures
like W. E. B. Dubois and Martin Luther King, Jr.[256]
Denominations for centuries attempted to bring the
church to a more spiritual functioning and doctrine
notably by Wesley, but it was Seymour (from Louisiana)
who actually accomplished it, birthing the Church of
God in Christ and the Assemblies of God. Pentecostals
combined are the second largest Christian group second
only behind the Catholic church. They are dominantly
the fastest growing movement in the world, particularly
in the global south: Africa, Latin America and Southeast

---

[256] "Pentecostalism: William Seymour...... | Christian History
...."
https://www.christianitytoday.com/history/issues/issue-65/pe
ntecostalism-william-seymour.html.

Asia but just in 113 short years. To describe it would be like describing the Big Bang. Creation was a big bang. The resurrection of Jesus Christ was a big bang. Pentecost was a big bang and Seymour released this bang around the world stating that all Christians should be baptized in the Holy Ghost with the evidence of speaking in tongues. Seymour was a student of Charles Parham, who also believed, but split with Seymour over interracial congregations. The Assemblies of God broke off from the Church of God in Christ (COGIC) a decade after Bishop Charles Harrison Mason began COGIC because of racism.

The leader of the Canadian Church of God in Christ, Bishop Clarence Leslie Morton used the media to reach thousands with an international radio broadcast. His youngest son left Canada and began pastoring Greater St. Stephen which was a baptist church in New Orleans. He founded a movement (the Full Gospel Baptist Church Fellowship) in 1993 adding balance, giving baptists the right to choose tongues or not. Creation was a big bang but the next big bang was the resurrection and Pentecost combined, being one big bang. Augustine penned: "You stir man to take pleasure in praising you, because you have made us for yourself, and our heart is restless until it finds its rest in you." Our triune selves, mind, body, spirit cannot rest until we find the triune Him where balance is critical to enter the spiritual realm and leave the passions and desires (dopaminergic stimulation) of ourselves. The 12th doctrinal distinctive describes "that it is God's desire that all believers live their lives under the control of, or being continuously filled with the Holy Ghost. We believe there are many fillings and there is to be the ongoing filling ministry of the Spirit in the life of the believer for empowerment to effectively and victoriously live a life that glorifies God". This balance sees men under God's power allowing women in ministry as co-equal in the spirit, but building the man in his church, family and community role along with building the woman in her church, family and community role. His wife, Dr. Debra B. Morton now pastors Greater St. Stephen. This balance ushered in a genre of music and praise holistically as music reaches every part of our being. The music is flush with New

Orleans' back beats reminiscent of the Bamboula beat from Africa. The holistic experience of spiritual power permeates and empowers every aspect of a believer's second by second life, bringing power over serotonin/dopamine imbalances that manifests in personal self destructive behavior and selfish community destroying behaviors.

All church doctrines create a framework, but the heart must receive the ultimate truth to have power. The more the church doctrine leads congregants to monotheistic worship by faith, the easier the attack is on their passions. Passions drive selfishness.

The issue today is similar to the argument over the Nicene Creed which is a statement of beliefs. The view of the trinity forms the basis of Christian doctrine. Beginning in 325 to quell doctrinal arguments the creed was created but controversies remain which separated the westerns and eastern churches until this day along with the north/south split. Many Protestant denominations adopted the creed also. The question is

which roles do the Father, Son and Holy Spirit have?
Did the son come from the Father? The First Council of
Nicea didn't include the Holy Spirit at all. The
Baptist/Pentecostal divisions are caused by a similar
argument. Most doctrinal controversies are derived
from the question of what is the balance of the trinity.
Why is this so important? Our spirit must be strong
enough to overcome feelings or else behavioral change
must come from legalism by fear. Spiritual power
comes from faith in God. An unbalanced view of the
Godhead (Trinity) weakens our faith and seers our
conscious leading to feelings taking over: racism. It
must be spirit over mind. Passions are strong. Fears are
monsters. Sex dominates. Faith in God overcomes those
passions creating the fruit of joy, peace, gentleness, and
self control.

History fails in its ability to describe the horrendous
effects of war on church doctrine and denominational
organization. We could only imagine how church
leaders responded to wartime church, something
America hasn't seen fully since the lynchings of post

reconstruction and slavery. Mass incarceration is horrible but more hidden. How mass incarceration is affecting church doctrine remains to be studied. Obviously the reduction in black male availability with 8 males per every 10 females affects all aspects of culture but more research is needed to fully understand the doctrinal effects. In many neighborhoods the figure is 3 men for every 5 black women while the white population is near the optimal 1 to 1 ratio.[257] Technology has unleashed passions that are destroying us all. Racism is unabated and increasing. Sugar and refined carbohydrate addictions are just another symptom of a distracted mind. Passions and feelings seek pleasures. The stresses of racism and poverty exacerbate the distractions where we lose focus on who we are. Dr. Robert Lustig looked to neurobiology and created the 4 C's to reset our mental balance: Connect, Contribute, Cope and Cook. Focusing on these 4 C's restores our dopamine/serotonin balance. Dopamine is

---

[257] "The Mass Incarceration of Black Men Has Created a Gender ...."
https://www.governing.com/topics/public-justice-safety/gov-black-men-gender-imbalance-population.html.

the reward neurotransmitter while serotonin is the contentment neurotransmitter. Too much dopamine leads to addictions and drives down serotonin, leading to depression. Dopamine is "I me my" while serotonin is "we". To reset our neurotransmitter balance we should focus on connecting with others and only by "eye to eye". Social media and cell phones don't work. The body responds through mirror neurons when we connect in person. Altruistic giving and not taking restores balance in our minds. The key is giving without expecting anything in return; no quid pro quo or give to get. Next is to cope. Cope through exercise, sleep, disconnecting from screens and multitasking. The modern cell phone is a dopamine volcano. His last C is to cook. Rarely will you find a restaurant that doesn't serve added sugars or refined carbohydrates. Even vegan restaurants usually sell meals full of added sugars. We have to cook. He stresses omega 3's and foods with tryptophan which is a serotonin precursor. We definitely must eliminate free sugars. He became famous through a YouTube video describing sugar as toxic.[258] It made waves with such a detailed description of the toxic effects of sugar.[259]

Dr. Lustig isn't a Christian but his neurobiological theory is so biblical (church). And yes science will challenge the mechanisms and find other neurotransmitters other than dopamine but don't expect the effects to change, as that is how passions work.

The body demands balance and to truly achieve it, our faith must be in one God and "thou shalt have no other gods before me". True monotheism has always led to peace. Monotheism "in name only" is worse than anything. God is real. Science is becoming used to finding these emergent phenomena as the more it learns, the bigger the questions get with only theology and philosophy offering answers. Philosophy must always succumb to theology to move society forward.

---

[258] "http://youtu.be/dBnniua6-oM - Hannah Frances Milward ...." https://www.facebook.com/PTAGlobalCommunity/posts/httpyoutub edbnniua6-om/212694942082198/.

[259] "The 4Cs | Robert Lustig Website." https://robertlustig.com/4cs/.

The physician then has an opportunity to connect with the patient's true advisor: their pastor. Britain has taken the lead in social prescribing where physicians prescribe social connections to benefit patients.[260] The church is the optimum place for people to build connections but Britain's NHS is taking a major step forward into entering the lives of the patient. The model is very good for the unchurched but for patients with pastors (PMP), doctors just need to encourage them to connect with their pastors. The church is the God designed model with the Bible as the policy and procedure manual. It contains best practices, historical references, illustrations and future plans. It is the ultimate health and wellness book and the church is the perfect public health model. The church is designed by God to meet the holistic needs of the human mind, body, and spirit. Churches are perfect for building lasting relationships, mental peace, deliverance from evil, mentoring and family structure. Phillip Pizzo suggested that physicians should prescribe a system for

---

[260] "Re: Social prescribing: coffee mornings, singing ... - The BMJ."
https://www.bmj.com/content/363/bmj.k4857/rr-0.

patients, offering and encouraging: having a purpose, seeking social engagement, and fostering wellness through positive lifestyle choices because they are important in reducing morbidity and mortality and improving the life journey.[261] What Pizzo described in this 2020 JAMA article was just a good church. No other system could create what he envisioned. The added benefit of church is that in contrast to connecting with strangers, church has naturally occurring relationships which are much more powerful than anything (non church) social prescribing could create. [262] An editor of the British Medical Journal invited me to respond to an article by Ann Robinson on social prescribing. The BMJ is truly taking the lead in this paradigm shift in medicine but Britain is one of the most non religious countries in the world. They just need churches with stronger pastors. Imagine social prescribing being the fuel to blend church and

[261] "A Prescription for Longevity in the 21st Century - JAMA Network." 9 Jan. 2020, https://jamanetwork.com/journals/jama/fullarticle/2758735.

[262] "Social relationships and mortality risk: a meta-analytic ... - NCBI." 27 Jul. 2010, https://www.ncbi.nlm.nih.gov/pubmed/20668659.

medicine. Dreams take teams.[263] God is up to something through science.

http://www.tinyurl.com/y2j3wmad

In conclusion, greater health can be achieved by overcoming the forces of disease. These forces have deep historical roots. By recognizing these forces and their histories we can identify and overcome. The "doctor • patient • pastor" triad is a powerful health building model. Let's step into the future as a team.

---

[263] "Re: Social prescribing: coffee mornings, singing ... - The BMJ." https://www.bmj.com/content/363/bmj.k4857/rr-0.

Physicians

1. Allow patients with pastors (PMP) to use the resources the church has available.
2. Pastoral inspiration and encouragement is a powerful vehicle for behavioral change.
3. The pastor's role can be seen as a family member where patients have full control of their level of access.
4. By definition, all pastors are able to inspire behavioral change.
5. The best practices model is the social prescribing model.[264]
6. The physician's role is passive.

Frequently asked questions

1. What is the physician's liability?
   ○ Patient self-referral does not create liability.

---

[264] "Social prescribing in the US and England: Emerging ...." https://sirenetwork.ucsf.edu/tools-resources/resources/social-prescribing-us-and-england-emerging-interventions-address-patients. Accessed 9 Dec. 2019.

2. How do I know if a patient has a pastor?

    o The physician's role is passive. The patient has the responsibility to communicate all information and desires.

3. What is the physician's role?

    o Awareness and education.

4. What if the patient asks if it is a good idea?

    o It's personal between the patient and their pastor and depends upon the strength of the relationship.

5. What are the risks?

    o Toxic pastor/member relationships. This should be a concern in any relationship that the patient may have including spouse, children, family or work.

6. How do I control my own biases?

    o Religion creates biases but the patient has free will to decide. The relationships are already established and outside of the medical system's area of power. Free will is the key.

7. Should I discuss my beliefs?

- Depending upon the strength of the relationship but always being aware of the power differential. All people struggle with beliefs and the beliefs of a physician can greatly influence a patient.

8. What is the goal?
   - Allowing the patient to use every tool available to improve health including their pastor.

Technology makes almost all information quickly available. The question is who does a patient trust? It is imperative to allow the patient to connect with the person they greatly trust to help them achieve behavioral change. Patients with pastors (PWP) have a distinct advantage in life by having an ally in behavioral change.[265] [266] [267]

---

[265] "PubMed - NCBI."
https://www.ncbi.nlm.nih.gov/pubmed/25119627.
[266] "Leading their flocks to health? Clergy health and the ... - NCBI." https://www.ncbi.nlm.nih.gov/pubmed/23718954.
[267] "The role of religious leaders in promoting healthy ... - NCBI." https://www.ncbi.nlm.nih.gov/pubmed/23516019.

The two facets of this approach are the measurable targets (with form) provided by the member's own physician and secondly the QSS Program which has been shown to reduce waist circumference by an average of 8.19% and weight by 4.69% in 40 days. The process was designed with a goal of creating a simple, easy to adopt, educational tool for the patient that lasts a lifetime. For it to be easy to adopt it had to be culturally sensitive. It has to meet the Thanksgiving test. A person can eat or prepare a QSS meal for Thanksgiving without looking weird or being rejected. They would just have to replace the drinks with water, tea or flavored water just as families do when they refuse to provide alcohol to their guests. They just refuse unhealthy drinks. Whole grains are really easy to adopt. Whole grains will fit right in everyone's cultural dishes. When cooked correctly people love it.

Liability is always a concern and being passive solves it but we hope the United States adopts a social prescribing type system such as what the NHS has in Britain. Patients are referred to all types of social organizations but the church is perfect for everything social prescribing aspires to achieve. It would create the liability infrastructure needed for active physician referrals to a patient's pastor. Morally and ethically, a physician should be free to actively encourage a patient to work with their pastor on behavioral change.

The Role of the Pastor

1. Recognize the power of the shepherd's role.

2. Everyone needs someone they can trust in their hearts to help them overcome addictions.

3. Understand "shared decision making". Physicians should share the decision making with the patient and their family (and/or pastor) on whether to prescribe certain medications depending upon risks or patient's motivation to change. A physician may ask: you can fill this prescription now or try to lose 3 inches off your waist first. Which will you decide? This is pastoral counseling at its best.

4. Use your tools and be open to develop new tools:

    a. Health Ministry

        i. Exercise programs

        ii. Healthy cooking classes

        iii. Health professional's speaking opportunities

        iv. Screenings

        v. Testimonies

      vi.   Support groups

   b. Counseling

      i.   Be holistic: mind, body and spirit.

      ii.   Know limitations in mind and body.

   c. Wield the powerful tool of grace

      i.   Grace overcomes condemnation and guilt.

      ii.   Fat shaming is real and destructive. Grace is the most powerful weapon against condemnation.

5. Your personal health can be private

   a. You don't have to give your testimony.

   b. Your job is to build up others.

   c. Know you are valuable and can help.

   d. Know that perfect health doesn't exist and we are all striving to be better.

   e. Know exterior results may not match internal realities.

6. Know diseases are extremely complex

   a. Lifestyle is only a part.

   b. We only see a part of lifestyle.

c. There are many other factors including but not limited to genetics and other environmental factors.

d. Guidelines change regularly as science always ends with a question.

7. Ethics is paramount

a. Flow with the physician and the entire healthcare team, not against them.

b. Don't add to or take away from the physician's plan.

c. Don't offer herbs or supplements that worked for you ever.

d. Don't recommend your diet or superfoods.

e. If you believe the patient is being ill advised by her physician, consult with a healthcare professional to see if your concerns are valid before speaking to the patient.

f. Always encourage members to take their medications as prescribed. The goal is to where possible decrease medications but always, always as directed by the physician.

g. Be aware that millions of people die early because they believe prayer will heal them and don't need medicine or surgery. They need to be made aware of Luke's role on Jesus's team.

8. Recognize that all diseases are not caused by sin. All diseases are not caused by ignorance.

9. Use extreme caution in delegating to associate ministers. The pastor's role is spiritual and even church health professional's direct participation in counseling faces numerous ethical and logistical challenges. The best practice is to keep the focus spiritual. Everyone eats so it is easy for people to not comprehend the challenges when dealing with disease, diet and medications.

10. Remember to keep the focus on encouraging behavioral change based upon the doctor's plan... Each team member has a role and all must work together to benefit the patient/member.

Pastors have access to the hearts and minds of the members usually at least weekly to shape their God consciousness... We are available for counseling sessions and to join in with activities. The shepherd's role is the power role in behavioral change. The benefits are endless including better mental health, longer life, a healthier body, less disease and more energy.

The Role of the Doctor

Sugar, porn and "likes" from social media has changed the culture to create a dopaminergic torrent. The unexposed elderly are dealing with children and grandchildren whose lives and lifestyles are foreign to those just a generation removed. Even many elderly are exposed to what Dr. Robert Lustig calls the "hacking of the American mind". Allowing this subgroup, patients with pastors (PWP), to use their already established church resources to help with behavioral change truly empowers the patient. Literally all pastors are experts at encouragement and motivation and would be excited to freely assist their members to meet those goals. Filling out the form provided to set goals is all that is needed. The patient's relationship with their pastor will guide everything else.

The QSS Program is optional and is designed to easily fit into the patient's lifestyle and culture. We studied 40 day commitments which gives patients an illustration.

Dr. Kevin Hall of the NIDDK stated in a tweet that the effects of ultra processed food restricted diets probably are the result of eliminating free sugars and refined carbohydrates. This is the basis for QSS. In a study of 37000 adults, Shan et al. found that carbohydrate quantity had no bearing on mortality but carbohydrate quality significantly affected mortality.[268] Low carb and ketogenic diets also have long term concerns and are challenging to maintain while they also require a huge cultural adjustments. Calorie counting and low fat diets also require huge cultural adjustments. 33% to 39% of bariatric surgery patients require hospitalization for complications within 5 years.[269] Almost any culture can easily make the QSS ingredient adjustments which allows families and friends to eat together and it drives the focus to whole, real, high quality foods. It's designed to be simple, simple, simple: Quit sodas, juices,

---

[268] "Association of Low-Carbohydrate and Low-Fat Diets With ...." 21 Jan. 2020, https://jamanetwork.com/journals/jamainternalmedicine/fullarticle/2759134.
[269] "Interventions and Operations 5 Years After Bariatric Surgery in ...." 15 Jan. 2020, https://jamanetwork.com/journals/jamasurgery/fullarticle/2758646.

smoothies and diet drinks. Switch to brown from white and Sweat everyday....

QSS...Quit-Switch-Sweat.

Appendix

Physician Form

Dear Doctor,

    Am I eligible to reduce any of my medications if I meet certain targets? _____yes_____no

If yes, please provide the applicable targets. I may also use this information to enlist the help and support of my family and/or my pastor to reach these targets.

High Blood Pressure Target:
Systolic_____
Diastolic_____
Consistently over _____Duration

Blood Sugar Target:
HbA1c_____
Time in Range_____
SMBG_____
Other_____
Consistently over _____ Duration

Cholesterol Target:
HDL_____
LDL_____
TG_____
Consistently over_____ Duration

Weight:_____
Consistently over_____ Duration

Waist Circumference:_____
Consistently over_____ Duration

Pastor Form

Dear Pastor,

I desire to reach certain health goals and I request your spiritual support. Please keep all of my health information confidential unless I give permission in writing to release it.

I would like to meet:

Weekly_____
Monthly_____
Quarterly_____

My choice of communication is:

Phone_____
In Person_____
Text_____

I would like to be a part of group where we can all work together:

Is there one available?_____

If not can one be created?_____

I need spiritual help in avoiding:

Sweets_____   Other_____

Sodas_____